This is a guide to over four hundred bird-watching spots
in England, Scotland and Wales.

Everyone, expert and beginner alike, will find this book
indispensable. It tells you how to get there, where to go when
you are on the site, the species to look out for at different
seasons, the times of high tides, whose permission to ask,
where permits are obtainable, whether accommodation is
available.

The book is fully illustrated with maps to guide the visitor
to the public footpaths and the best access and observation
points.

'Mr. Gooders has produced an admirably practical, well-
mapped guide, county by county, to the chief areas of
feathered interest in Great Britain. The information is
succinctly given . . . clearly catalogued and indexed and
easy to get at.' – *Sunday Times*

'A good and, I think, a valuable book and one that will be
widely read and used.' – *Birds*

'Invaluable . . . It mentions the main species of each locality,
and tells you *precisely* how to get there.' – *Wildlife*

JOHN GOODERS is a Lecturer in Education and lives in
South London. He is a member of the London Natural
History Society, and a bird-watcher of boundless
enthusiasm. His activities have taken him the length and
breadth of Britain.

WHERE TO WATCH BIRDS

To all who have contributed
this book is gratefully dedicated.

JOHN GOODERS

Where to Watch Birds

Introduction by Roger Tory Peterson

SPHERE

SPHERE BOOKS LTD

30/32 Gray's Inn Road, London, W.C.1

First published in Great Britain in 1967 by
Andre Deutsch

© John Gooders, 1967
First Sphere Books edition, 1969
This is an abridged edition.
The unabridged hardcover edition is available
from Andre Deutsch, Limited, price 30/-
Set in 9 on 10 Times

TRADE MARK

SPHERE

Printed in Great Britain by
Cox & Wyman Ltd., London, Reading and Fakenham

Introduction

Bird-watching, bird-finding, bird-spotting, tick-hunting, or birding – call it what you will – has come of age. It is moving beyond the stage of identification guides into the era of Baedekers. North America has had such Baedekers since 1951 when Dr. Olin Sewall Pettingill, Jr., published his *Guide to Bird Finding East of the Mississippi* (Oxford University Press), and 1953 when he supplemented it with his *Guide to Bird Finding West of the Mississippi*.

Normally Great Britain, the mother country of the modern bird-watcher, is the first to launch a useful device or new tool, but perhaps the reason that this inevitable book has not appeared earlier is that the number of choice spots of ornithological interest in England, Wales and Scotland runs into the hundreds. Where does a compiler start? It took the encyclopaedic James Fisher to break the ice with his *Shell Nature Lover's Atlas* (1966) which gives capsule summaries of sites and areas of interest to the field naturalist (including those of every stripe and hue from paleontologists to beetle-watchers).

This new book by John Gooders, which has long been awaited by the field-glass fraternity, goes into depth on the birds, giving explicit directions for reaching many bird-rich areas and a breakdown by season of some of the species that might be seen.

How I wish I had owned such a guidebook when I was trying to fill in my own British list (I went years before I saw my first cirl bunting, finally shown me by Richard Fitter). Had I owned such a book I would not have waited until 1966 before 'discovering' Noss in the Shetlands (while on the Scottish cruise of the International Ornithological Congress). I intend to return to Noss for a week or two of photography some June, and in this guide Mr. Gooders informs me that the way to do it is to cross from Lerwick to Bressay, then taxi (or walk) 2½ miles to Noss Sound and summon the shepherd to row me across.

This valuable book will not only enhance the thoroughness of coverage of bird-spotting in Britain but it will also aid the conservationist in his perennial fight to preserve key wildlife areas against deterioration or outright destruction. The more people travel about to see birds the more they become a recreational resource to be reckoned with and to be preserved. As an example, I might point to a world-famous vantage point across the Atlantic — Hawk Mountain in Pennsylvania, where the hundreds of watchers on any October weekend may far outnumber the migrating birds of prey. The important by-products of this visitation have been the conversion of the local populace from hawk-shooters to hawk-watchers and the passing of protective legislation.

Birds with their high rate of metabolism and furious pace of living, demonstrate life forces perhaps better than any other animals. Like the canaries once used by miners to detect gas leakage, they may act as sensitive indicators of subtle (or drastic) environmental changes. Therefore the growing army of bird-watchers, which ranges all the way from enthusiastic *aficionados* to scientific ornithologists, has become an important watchdog over our environment.

ROGER TORY PETERSON

Contents

List of Maps

Addresses of National Organizations

BRITISH ORNITHOLOGISTS' UNION,
c/o The Bird Room, British Museum (Natural History), London
SW7

BRITISH ORNITHOLOGISTS' CLUB
As for the Union.

BRITISH TRUST FOR ORNITHOLOGY,
Beech Grove, Tring, Herts.

COUNCIL FOR NATURE,
41 Queens Gate, London SW7

NATURE CONSERVANCY,
England: 19 Belgrave Square, London SW1
Scotland: 12 Hope Terrace, Edinburgh 9
Wales: Penrhos Road, Bangor, Carns.

ROYAL SOCIETY FOR THE PROTECTION OF BIRDS,
The Lodge, Sandy, Beds.

SCOTTISH ORNITHOLOGISTS' CLUB,
21 Regent Terrace, Edinburgh 7

WILDFOWL TRUST,
Slimbridge, Glos.

Preface

The recent expansion of the number of bird-watchers is merely the visible tip of a national interest in birds, nature, and the countryside as a whole. A movement that is reflected in the rapid expansion of the membership of the Royal Society for the Protection of Birds and the popularity of television nature programmes. At the same time there has been a growth in the demands of other seekers after fresh air and field sports, notably sailing, fishing, shooting and water-skiing. Unfortunately, these activities sometimes serve to destroy what are ideal spots for the naturalist, or important scientific sites. More unfortunate, naturalists are unable to compete with sports whose participants are willing to pay large sums of money for facilities.

Industry and government frequently threaten, and sometimes destroy good sites. An area as important to naturalists as Dungeness has not been spared. The Cairngorms skiing hotels will want to attract visitors in summer as well as winter and the chair lift takes the public to the tops and dotterel territory for a few shillings. The beach at Minsmere is no long safe for little terns. Only by fully embracing the huge numbers of people that form the television audience of *Look* can naturalists hope to compete with other demands on the countryside.

Peterson, Mountfort and Hollom's *Field Guide* has made a key to identification readily available. I hope that this book too will encourage people to go out and see birds, join local societies, and become active supporters of the conservation movement. It will doubtless be argued that everything is being put on the plate for the beginner and that the pressure of watchers on certain well-known localities will increase. Though I hope for more watchers I also hope to tempt them, and the established expert, by accounts of places unknown. Even if this ideal fails and more and more watchers swarm to Cley I doubt whether it will create over-watching. More watchers go there than almost anywhere, yet there are still plenty of birds, including rare breeding species. I suppose Cley marshes are safe – or would someone like to build a fully fledged marina in Blakeney Harbour? Or would it be a good site for a nuclear power station? Or what about a storage depot for North Sea gas?

The pressure is on. If the choice is more watchers or more

marinas and commercial development most will surely prefer
to share their pleasures rather than be denied them altogether.

HOW TO USE THE GUIDE

Over five hundred places in England, Wales and Scotland are
described and grouped alphabetically in counties or county
groups in line with current ornithological practice. Counties
are arranged alphabetically, and brief details of local societies,
including the address of the current secretary, the address from
which publications are available, and to which reports should
be sent, and details of subscriptions are given together with the
titles of any particularly relevant books. The addresses are
always changing and the book will doubtless become out of
date in several instances before it is published. If societies can
arrange a permanent forwarding address for publication, perhaps through a museum or library, they will be doing the
nature movement a great service, with obvious benefits to
themselves. I would be pleased to receive any such addresses
for future revisions of this guide.

After each place name the Ordnance Survey (OS) one inch
map number is given, and this is followed where appropriate
by the high tide (HT) constant prefixed by a + or − and the
base point. This enables high tide on any occasion to be cal-
culated by reference to a current almanac like Whitakers or a
local paper.

The most interesting regular species are listed under seasonal
headings roughly in order of interest but with concessions to
family ties. Thus all waders are generally grouped together.
The entries show what is found at the different seasons;
though seasons are bird seasons and not human.

Detailed instructions on routes from the nearest large town
or trunk road should be read in conjunction with the appropriate Ordnance Survey one inch map, an indispensable aid to
the British bird-watcher. Access details including details of
how to obtain permits, plus help with local accommodation,
where relevant, follows. Access and permit details are always
changing, paths are being closed and new reserves created.
Though every effort has been made to check material there
will be mistakes. This is inevitable in a work of this kind where
information is supplied by so many people, and observers
should check locally all details of access to private property
before entering. Where permits are available they generally
have to be obtained well in advance of any visit.

In some areas the vast majority of watchers will be on holi-day and more general accounts, including a county or county group introduction, are given. This applies to the Scottish islands where the choice has deliberately been selective. Many wonderful places like the Shiants, the Bulgachs and North Rona have been omitted.

Very few abbreviations are used and are then readily understandable:

BTO   = British Trust for Ornithology
HT   = High Tide
NT   = Naturalists' Trust
OS   = Ordnance Survey
RSPB   = Royal Society for the Protection of Birds
WAGBI   = Wildfowlers' Association of Great Britain and
          Ireland

Apart from these abbreviations one or two pieces of ornithological shorthand (i.e. 'commic terns' for common and Arctic terns) have been used.

Part 1: England

Bedfordshire

THE LODGE, SANDY   OS 147

Situated 2 miles south-east of Sandy alongside the A603. It is
the headquarters of the RSPB and visitors are welcome. The
102 acres provide an attractive area of woodland and heath
supporting a wide range of common breeding birds. Two trails
are laid out for visitors, and all the usual RSPB bird accessor-
ies can be purchased.

SUMMER: nightjar, redstart, tree pipit, lesser spotted wood-
pecker, woodcock.

The reserve is open from 9 a.m. to 5 p.m.; on weekdays in
winter and all week in summer. Leave Sandy on the A603 and
the entrance is on the right after 1¾ miles.

WYBOSTON GRAVEL PIT   OS 134

The pit is 5 miles north of Sandy on the eastern side of the A1.
A large area of gravel excavation has created some quite extensive areas of open water that are frequented by a variety of
duck in winter. Bewick's swans are often noted and great crested grebes breed. Passage brings small numbers of the commoner waders as well as little ringed plovers.

WINTER: teal, pochard, goosander, Bewick's swan.

SPRING: garganey, little ringed plover.

SUMMER: great crested grebe.

AUTUMN: little ringed plover, terns.

A sign on the eastern side of the A1 1 mile south of Eaton
Socon directs the visitor to Wyboston Quarry. A straight lane
between two houses leads past cooling towers to the workings
and good views by casual visitors can be obtained from this.
Regulars should contact the Site Manager.

Berkshire, Buckinghamshire and Oxfordshire

FOXCOTE RESERVOIR (Bucks)   OS 146

The reservoir lies 2 miles north-east of Buckingham, immediately south of Foxcote Wood. It was flooded in 1956, covers
50 acres, and is a wildfowl refuge of the Berkshire, Bucking-
hamshire and Oxfordshire NT. Duck are undoubtedly the

Foxcote Reservoir: not shown on Ordance Survey map yet

main attraction, though watching for passage waders and terns
would probably be rewarding.

WINTER: wigeon, pintail, shoveler, pochard, tufted duck,
goosander.

SPRING: waders, terns.

SUMMER: great crested grebe.

AUTUMN: waders, terns.

HAM ISLAND BIRD SANCTUARY (BERKS)   OS 159

This is a marshy part of an old sewage farm lying 2 miles south-
east of Windsor on an island between two arms of the Thames
and covers 100 acres. The island and the surrounding water
are used by numbers of wildfowl, especially in hard weather.
Waders on passage are more reliable.

WINTER: Canada goose.

SPRING: green and common sandpipers.

SUMMER: yellow wagtail.

AUTUMN: ringed plover, green and wood sandpipers, dunlin.

The Sanctuary is managed by the Middle-Thames Natural
History Society, permits are obtainable from the Warden, 24
Queen's Close, Old Windsor. Leave the A308 eastwards on the
northern edge of Old Windsor and follow OS.

LAMBOURN DOWNS (Berks) OS 158

These hills are the eastern extension of the Marlborough Downs. They are ploughed chalklands rising to almost 800 feet, lying on either side of the B4001 north of Lambourn village near Hungerford. Typical chalkland birds include stone curlew and cirl bunting. There are always heavy passages of wheatears and, out of the breeding season, a variety of raptors are noted. Though not regular, the latter include the occasional harrier.

WINTER: golden plover, stonechat, corn bunting.
SPRING: wheatear.
SUMMER: stone curlew, wheatear, whinchat, corn and cirl buntings.
AUTUMN: turtle dove, wheatear.

Leave the A4 at Newbury and follow the B4000 to Lambourn. The B4001 leads northwards over the downs and there are numerous tracks and paths to the north that are rights of way.

VIRGINIA WATER (Berks) OS 169

The lake lies north of the A30, 2½ miles south-west of Egham. The water covers 130 acres with several long arms stretching to north and west. Its wildfowl population includes quite large numbers of mandarin ducks and garganey are regular on passage. The surrounding mixed woodland holds interesting breeding species.

WINTER: mandarin duck, wigeon, shoveler, pochard, tufted duck, goosander, smew, siskin, goldcrest.
SPRING: garganey.
SUMMER: great crested grebe, mandarin duck, warblers, woodpeckers, hawfinch, woodcock.

Stop on the A30, 3 miles west of the Thames at Egham before the Wheatsheaf Hotel. The lake can be seen on the right of the road. Access unrestricted.

WINDSOR GREAT PARK (Berks) OS 159 and 169

The Park is immediately south of Windsor and the A332 runs through its north-western corner. It covers a huge area of predominantly open parkland with plantations and coverts of coniferous and deciduous trees. To the northwest, outside the park proper, lies Windsor Forest. The Great Meadow Pond is an excellent centre for wildfowl, including mandarin and passage garganey, and there are frequent hobbys in summer.

WINTER: wigeon, shoveler, pochard, mandarin duck.
SPRING: garganey.

SUMMER: hobby, nightjar, woodpeckers, grasshopper, reed and wood warblers, tree pipit.

Leave Windsor southwards on the A332 for direct access to the Park. Turn right on to the B383 alongside Windsor Forest.

Cambridgeshire

BRECKLAND   OS 135 and 136

Breckland lies roughly in the rectangle between Mildenhall, Bury St. Edmunds, Watton and Methwold and covers parts of three counties. As it lies within 20 miles of Cambridge, it receives full cover from the University and is most fully reported in the Cambridge Bird Club Report. The last hundred years have seen the former sandy wastes turned into areas of productive farming and forestry. Over half is now coniferous forest of varying age and comparatively few large areas of open heath remain.

Nevertheless, the Brecks are good for birds and the traditional species are still found, though often in changed habitats. Stone curlew now breed on agricultural land while the other speciality the crossbill, has benefited from the planting of conifers. Amongst the best remaining heaths, East Wretham belongs to the Norfolk NT and includes the two important meres of Langmere and Ringmere. The Trust also owns Thetford and Weeting Heaths, which are National Nature Reserves and there is a further National Nature Reserve at Cavenham Heath, access to which is partly restricted. The RSPB's Reserves at Horn and Weather Heaths are totally restricted.

The mere at Livermere Park holds an interesting variety of wildfowl and the heathland meres often hold Bewick's swans and goosander.

WINTER: Bewick's swan, goosander, shoveler, brambling, siskin.

SUMMER: gadwall, shoveler, Canada goose, ringed plover, snipe, redshank, curlew, stone curlew, long-eared and short-eared owls, nightjar, woodlark, willow tit, wheatear, whinchat, redstart, nightingale, grasshopper warbler, goldcrest, red-backed shrike, siskin, redpoll, crossbill.

The whereabouts of unusual breeding species is unlikely to be disclosed but interesting birds can be found with searching. The following are among the better spots:

1. LIVERMERE: leave the A143 3 miles north of Bury and half a mile north of Great Barton northwards to Great Livermere. Take the lane to the Church. There is generally no

objection to bird-watchers walking along the main track to the mere, provided one keeps to the footpath.

2. RIVER LARK AND CAVENHAM HEATH: leave Bury northwards on the A1101 to Icklingham. Past the village and a quarter of a mile past the junction with the B1112 turn left on a track to Temple Bridge. General access along river and over heath.

3. BRANDON SAWMILL: leave Brandon northwards on the A1065. Between the fork on the northern side of the level crossing is an old pine wood which is worth a look.

4. EAST WRETHAM: leave Thetford northwards on the A11 and fork left after 1¾ miles. Stop near Ringmere and explore, especially the old pines to the west.

THE OUSE WASHES   OS 135

When the Fenland south of the Wash was drained, large new cuts were dug to speed the flow of water to the sea. Even these, however, were liable to flood in winter and so 'washes' were created on all of the major rivers. Quite simply they consist of two high walls set some distance apart, usually less than a mile, with the river running between the banks. In times of flood the river is simply allowed to overflow in this limited region and not here and there over the entire Fenland. The Ouse Washes are the largest and have recently been the only ones to flood regularly, indeed the Nene Washes have been ploughed and put to agricultural use.

The Ouse Washes most often flood in February and March, though they attract wildfowl throughout the winter whenever there is water. The section between Welney and Pymore always floods first and is thus the first area that bird-watchers visit. Next to flood are the Welney–Denver and Mepal–Pymore sections, whilst the Earith Mepal section only floods in the most exceptional circumstances. The whole provides a bird-watching locality 20 miles long by about threequarters of a mile wide. There is also an outlying area between Over and Earith that floods occasionally. Though at first such a vast area seems unmanageable there are numerous access points.

Wildfowl are the main attraction with Bewick's swan and pintail as the centrepieces. Up to one third of the total British population of this duck and over 800 Bewick's swans have been counted. Such numbers are often lost amongst the hordes of other wildfowl. Though surface feeding duck are most numerous, even sawbills are occasionally present in good numbers. Whooper swans are noted every year.

Should there be a freeze-up, the stretch of river between Denver and Wiggenhall provides excitement.

The Ouse Washes provide 20 miles of outstanding ornithological interest. In exceptionally hard winters, when the whole of this area is deserted, the river north of Denver is sometimes very exciting

WINTER: (When flooded, usually February–March): Bewick's swan, pintail, wigeon, teal, pochard, tufted duck, shoveler, golden plover, ruff, winter thrushes, short-eared owl.

The whole of the area can be worked from either eastern or western banks but crossing from one to the other is only possible where road bridges cross the river. In practice most watchers work the area from the western bank which is the first to flood. The best main road is the A10 between Cambridge and Kings Lynn and a start is made from this at Littleport. Each section is then dealt with in order of flooding, so that watchers keeping to the route as outlined will know that they have covered all the floods when they arrive at a dry area. It should be remembered that all fields are privately owned and are private shoots, though there are now three nature reserves owned by the RSPB and the Wildfowl Trust.

1. WELNEY-PYMORE (first to flood): turn westwards at Littleport on to the A1101. After 4 miles this turns northwards beside the Hundred Foot Drain and a large embankment. Turn left over the suspension bridge and continue across the Ouse Washes to Welney. Walk southwards between the two cuts on a high wall giving first class views over the Washes to the east. Walk 2 miles and return.

2. DENVER-WELNEY (second to flood): as for section 1, but turn northwards at Welney along embankment.

3. MEPAL-PYMORE (second to flood): leave Sutton Gault eastwards to Sutton. Turn left on the B1381 and in 1 mile turn left on the A142 to Mepal. Continue across the Washes, here at their narrowest point and walk northwards between the cuts on the western embankment.

4. MEPAL-EARITH (last to flood): leave Welney westwards turning left past the inn on to the B1100. After numerous right-angled turns, which should be taken left and right alternately, turn left at the B1098 and continue south to Chatteris. Turn left then right on to the A141, then quickly left again on to the B1050. In 1 mile turn left and follow a narrow road to Sutton Gault. Park on western side of Washes and explore to the south along high embankment between cuts.

5. Return to Sutton, then B1381 to the southern end of the Washes, where the floods to the south can be seen from the A1123.

WICKEN SEDGE FEN   OS 135
Wicken Fen is a last small remnant of the ancient vegetation of the Fens that has been maintained by its owners, the National Trust, by delicate manipulation of the water level. The area is

an impenetrable wilderness of sedges, reeds and thorn, intersected by wide rides along which visitors walk.

A mere of 10 acres was excavated on the neighbouring Adventurer's Fen in 1955, and the whole declared a sanctuary in 1957. The area is attractive at all seasons but principally in winter for duck, and in summer for breeding marsh birds.

WINTER: wigeon, shoveler, bittern, bearded tit.

SUMMER: great crested grebe, grasshopper warbler, long-eared owl.

The fen is reached from either the A142 westwards, or the A10 eastwards on to the B1085. The village of Wicken lies roughly half-way between these roads. At the western end of the village turn southwards for 300 yards down a track marked 'Wicken Fen'. A cottage on the left belongs to the warden who should be informed of arrival. Entrance is free but a key to the watch tower costs 1s. 0d. plus 10s. 0d. returnable deposit. This is an essential as it is the only way to see the mere.

Cheshire

DEE ESTUARY AND HILBRE ISLAND
OS 100, 108, and 109: HT — 0:17 Liverpool

The Cheshire-Flintshire border runs down the middle of the Dee Estuary, and it divides what are undoubtedly the two best bird-watching localities in the area between England and Wales. Shotton Pools, though on the right bank of the Dee are in Flint, and the islands at Hilbre are in Cheshire. The Dee at low tide is a huge shallow expanse 12 miles by 5 miles. Recent years have seen a considerable growth of salting along the eastern bank and this will doubtless hasten the almost continuous process of reclamation. Wildfowl are numerous here but are mainly found in the upper estuary on the secure middle banks. They include a flock of up to 1,000 pintail, which is but a fraction of previous concentrations.

During passage and winter the estuary is alive with waders, including immense flocks of knot and oystercatcher as well as most of the other species found regularly in Britain. At high tide most of the waders flight to the islands at Hilbre which have become much used by bird photographers.

Hilbre Island, Little Hilbre Island and Little Eye lie at the mouth of the Dee just off the Cheshire shore. They have been the site of a bird observatory and are now a reserve covering 5,750 acres. Though thronged by tourists in summer, they are deserted for the rest of the year. Apart from the waders regular species include divers, grebes, snow bunting, gulls (including glaucous in many years) in winter; and skuas, shearwaters, gannet, fulmar, terns, auks and passerines on migration.

Nearby on the mainland at West Kirby, the Marine Lake can hold interesting duck in hard weather, while the Red Rocks promontory on the north-eastern corner of the Dee is good for waders and duck at high tide.

WINTER: pintail, wigeon, shelduck, eider, knot, oystercatcher, godwits, purple sandpiper, divers, grebes, glaucous gull, snow bunting.

SPRING: waders, terns, passerines.

AUTUMN: waders, terns, skuas, shearwaters, auks, gannet, passerines.

Unless one is content to peer over miles of saltings there are very few places around the Dee that are worth visiting and there are certainly none to compare with the West Kirby–Hilbre area. The islands can be reached on foot from West Kirby, leaving there 3 hours before high tide at the latest. It is best to walk to Little Eye (the smallest and southernmost of the three) and then northwards along the rocks to the main island. Permits are needed for the main island only and are obtainable from the Hoylake UDC, Hoylake, Wirral, Cheshire. For photographers Little Eye is recommended.

MACCLESFIELD FOREST AND LANGLEY
RESERVOIRS   OS 110

This is an area of mainly coniferous plantations, some 2 miles square, lying 3 miles south-east of Macclesfield. Immediately east of the village of Langley are three small reservoirs, two of which lie in the forest and are surrounded by trees. Wildfowl are regular in some variety. The forest is best worked in summer though the specialities can be seen in winter as well. The view from Shutlingsloe (1,659 feet) to the southeast is panoramic.

WINTER: goldeneye, wigeon, great crested grebe, blackcock, goldcrest.

SUMMER: blackcock, goldcrest, willow tit, redstart, golden plover, red grouse.

Leave Macclesfield southwards on the A523 but turn left to Langley on unclassified roads in the suburbs. In the centre of Langley fork left past the reservoir, then right alongside another, then turn left to the third. Public footpaths lead through the forest in various directions, but go south up to Shutlingsloe.

MERSEY ESTUARY   OS 109; HT +0:30 Liverpool

Near its mouth the Mersey is not only narrow and deep but

flanked to both east and west by the industrial complex of Liverpool and Birkenhead. Further inland the river widens out and the industrial development is less dominating. The whole of this upper estuary empties out at low water leaving huge areas of mud along the southern bank. This coincides with the only area of fresh marshes on the Mersey. The Manchester Ship Canal acts as a barrier to casual disturbance.

Thousands of wildfowl are present in winter, including large but variable numbers of pintail. Bewick's swans and white-fronted geese (about a hundred) are more or less regular. Waders are present throughout the year in large numbers and the area of fresh marshes holds a wide range of the more usual migrant species.

WINTER: wigeon, pintail, shoveler, Bewick's swan, white-fronted goose, knot, curlew, short-eared owl.

SPRING AND AUTUMN: ruff, golden plover, curlew, knot.

Access to the estuary proper involves crossing the Manchester Ship Canal on to the 8 mile stretch of saltings and mud banks between the canal and the Mersey. Leave Chester on the A5116 to Moston and join the A41 westwards. After a little more than a mile, fork right on to the A5032 to Ellesmere Port. Pass under the railway bridge, turn right, and after passing over the Shropshire Union Canal, turn right again over railway lines on to the Ellesmere-Ince industrial road. Corridor Road turns off to the left to Stanlow Ferry (MSC). Permits must be obtained for any visit from the Manchester Ship Canal Co, 2 King Street, Manchester 3, and also from the Frodsham Wildfowlers' Club, if required during the shooting season (contact the Honorary Secretary, 'Meadowside', Royleen Drive, Frodsham, via Warrington, Cheshire).

ROSTHERNE MERE   OS 101
Rostherne is the most famous of the Cheshire meres; it lies between Altrincham and Knutsford, and is threequarters of a mile by half a mile. It is of glacial origin and is deep, providing little food for the hordes of wildfowl that have made it famous. It is fringed by woodland, willow beds and stretches of reeds.

Rostherne Mere is of national importance as a refuge for wildfowl, indeed the 4,000 mallard that are found there form what is probably the largest regular flock in Britain (see Loch of Strathbeg). The Mere also acts as a large gull roost that reaches an annual peak of over 20,000 in mid-winter.

Passage periods often bring numbers of commic and black terns, while an interesting variety of birds breed.

WINTER: mallard, teal, wigeon, pochard, tufted duck, shoveller, Canada goose, great crested grebe.

SPRING: commic and black terns.

SUMMER: hawfinch, woodcock, reed warbler.

AUTUMN: commic and black terns, water rail.

Access to the area by permit is strictly controlled by the Nature Conservancy. Since 1962 the A. W. Boyd Memorial Observatory has been open to the public by permit, which is obtainable from Mr. W. Mulligan, 432 Parrs Wood Road, Manchester 20, Lancs, price 5s. 0d. and stamped addressed envelope. Mr. Mulligan will give full details of route.

The Observatory is well equipped and gives first rate views over the Mere.

TATTON PARK MERE   OS 101

The Mere lies in Tatton Park immediately north of Knutsford to the west of the M6 and within 2 miles of the famous Rostherne Mere. The area was bequeathed by the late Lord Egerton to the National Trust which, together with the County Council, runs the Hall and Park. The Mere is 1 mile long by a quarter of a mile wide and the south-eastern corner is bordered by a small mixed wood. Wilfowl are numerous and varied and black terns are regular double passage migrants. The Hall itself is worth a visit.

WINTER: mallard, wigeon, tufted duck, pochard, teal, shoveler, goldeneye, Bewick's swan, Canada goose, cormorant.

SPRING: black tern.

SUMMER: great crested grebe, tufted duck, teal.

AUTUMN: black tern.

Leave Knutsford northwards on the A50 and fork right on to the A5034 in 2 miles. Take the second on the right along the park boundary and enter by the northern entrance. Opening hours vary according to the season but it is only open at weekends during the winter from 11 a.m. till about dusk.

Cornwall

FAL ESTUARY   OS 190; HT at Falmouth

The estuary stretches inland 8 miles to Truro. The main channel is deep with little foreshore and birds are concentrated in the side creeks that are like a series of small estuaries. The best are Devoran Creek, Tresillian River, Truro River and the Fal itself up to Ruan Lanihorne. All four are highly tidal and expose a good deal of mud. Though nowhere very wide their

twisting nature makes it very simple for the birds to fly quickly
out of sight when disturbed.

Wildfowl are not numerous though brent geese are occasionally present. Waders are frequent on passage and black-
tailed godwits and greenshank winter on the Tresillian and the
Fal.

WINTER: wigeon, teal, pintail, shoveler, merganser, black-
tailed godwit, greenshank.
SPRING: waders.
AUTUMN: black-tailed godwit, green sandpiper, spotted redshank, greenshank, curlew sandpiper.

The best access points are:

1. DEVORAN CREEK: leave Falmouth on the A39 and after
5 miles the road runs alongside the creek. Continue and take
the first right to Devoran and alongside the tidal area to
Penpoll.

2. TRURO RIVER: leave Truro southwards on the unclassified road running along the eastern side of the river to Mal-
pas.

3. TRESILLIAN RIVER: leave Truro southwards on unclassified roads to St. Clement. Keep left past the church and
continue alongside the river for 2 miles to Tresillian.

4. RIVER FAL: leave Truro eastwards on the A39 and half a
mile past Tresillian fork right on to A3078. After 4 miles
turn right at Tregony on to an unclassified road to Ruan
Lanihorne. Keep right at the church and view from the
road in half a mile. Take a maze of by-roads to Ardevora, 1
mile west-south-west of Ruan Lanihorne.

HAYLE ESTUARY   OS 189; HT −1:20 Milford Haven
The estuary is on the north coast near St. Ives, and is bordered
on the eastern side by Hayle and the A30. The mud flats are
little more than half a mile long and a quarter of a mile
across with a small growth of salt marsh.

The Carnsew Basin is separated from the main channel and
is the regular haunt of Slavonian grebes in winter. The nar-
rower eastern arm is worth a look but often more rewarding
are the artificial waters at its head. Sometimes a high tide
swamps the land at the head of the main estuary towards St.
Erth.

Winter waders include an occasional common sandpiper and
autumn passage brings a host of others, many of which use the
pools at the eastern end. All can be seen at close range and at

this time the Hayle is one of the best places for waders in the county.

WINTER: Slavonian grebe, wigeon, pintail, grey plover, common sandpiper, ruff.
AUTUMN: godwits, green sandpiper, spotted redshank, little stint, curlew sandpiper.

The main vantage point is the A30 which runs alongside the main part of the estuary. St. Ives is nearby, and an autumn holiday watching here and at St. Ives Island could be rewarding.

HELL'S MOUTH TO GODREVY POINT   OS 189
This is one of the most beautiful stretches of cliff coastline in Cornwall and is owned by the National Trust. Though the 5 miles of cliffs from Portreath to Godrevy Point are worth attention, this stretch involving Navax Point is the best. There are buzzards in the woods immediately south of Portreath.

SUMMER: razorbill, guillemot, raven, buzzard.

A track runs around the area making an excellent walk of about 3 miles. Leave the B3301, half a mile north of Gwithian on the north side of the Red River. A track runs away to the left out to Godrevy Point. The path to Hell's Mouth is about 1 mile further on along the B3301.

MARAZION MARSH   OS 189
Situated north of Mount's Bay, 2 miles east of Penzance, this marsh is one of the richest habitats in Cornwall. It is a submerged forest that is now a fresh marsh with reeds and shallow pools, and certainly a most attractive spot to any trans-Atlantic migrant. It is enclosed in a triangle formed by the main Penzance railway, the coast and the A394 along it, and the village of Marazion.

Passage waders are excellent both in spring and autumn, and almost anything else can, and does, turn up here. Divers and grebes are regular in winter and in particular both Slavonian and black-necked grebes are present.

WINTER: Slavonian and black-necked grebes, divers.
SPRING: garganey, waders.
SUMMER: reed warbler.
AUTUMN: jack snipe, wood sandpiper, ruff, rarities.

Leave Penzance eastwards on the A30 and after 2 miles bear right at Longrock on to the A394. Pass over the railway and drive along the shore road. Park and view the marsh over the stone wall, there is no general entry.

ST. AGNES HEAD   OS 185 and 189

On the north coast near St. Agnes and south of Perranporth.
The main attraction are the breeding sea birds.

SUMMER: kittiwake, razorbill, guillemot, raven.

Leave Redruth northwards on the A30 and turn westward at
the junction with the B3277 to St. Agnes. Continue straight on
past the Church on to the unclassified Beacon Drive. After 1
mile, and opposite St. Agnes Beacon, turn right out to New-
down's Head. Walk along cliff top to St. Agnes Head. Wear
stout footwear, there are adders in the area!

THE ISLES OF SCILLY   OS 189

The islands lie 28 miles west-south-west of Lands End and are
fully exposed to the rigours of the Atlantic. Yet the mildness
of their climate and especially the bland winters have made
them famous as producers of early flowers. Five islands are
inhabited: St. Mary's, Bryher, Tresco, St. Agnes and St. Martin's. From a bird-watcher's point of view only St. Mary's, Tresco, and St. Agnes are really worth spending a holiday on, and
of these, St. Mary's is so much the better served by transport
services that the general watcher need look no further. Of the
uninhabited islands Annet is outstanding but many others are
worth attention during the summer. The Western Rocks hold
razorbills, and Gorregan has a small colony of guillemots and
kittiwakes, these birds also breed on St. Helen's. Annet, however, has large breeding colonies of storm petrel, Manx shearwater, common and Arctic terns, puffin and gulls.

St. Mary's has a wealth of birds but is best during passage
periods, and rare herons are annual. All of the beaches hold
waders, and the rough marsh immediately east of Hugh Town
is interesting.

Tresco has the Great Pool which attracts waders, holds a
trans-Atlantic migrant at least once a year, and is the best
area in Scilly for wildfowl. The woodland areas are larger
than anywhere else in Scilly.

St. Agnes is the site of the Bird Observatory which is housed
in a farmhouse surrounded by the minute, high-hedged flower
fields. In autumn the island is as good as anywhere in Britain
for seeing unusual birds, American waders and gulls, and heavy
movements of sea birds.

The best sea-watching spot on the islands is Horse Point,
St. Agnes, but the best sea birds are seen from the *Scillonian*
between Hugh Town and Penzance. Regulars include sooty
shearwater, storm petrel, gannet, Sabine's gull, phalaropes,
and skuas.

SPRING: turnstone, sanderling, whimbrel, herons, shear-waters, gannet, warblers, chats.

SUMMER: Manx shearwater, storm petrel, kittiwake, puffin, razorbill, guillemot, gulls.

AUTUMN: waders, warblers, chats, flycatchers, firecrest, sooty shearwater, phalaropes, skuas, Sabine's gull.

The passage to Scilly is by RMMV *Scillonian* and RMMV *Queen of the Isles*, from Penzance, regular sailings and con-nections with overnight trains from London make it possible to be in Scilly 12 hours after leaving Paddington. There is also a BEA helicopter service from Penzance during the season, connecting with air services from other cities.

Launches connect with steamer services to all inhabited islands and also run from island to island at frequent intervals.

ST. AGNES BIRD OBSERVATORY offers hostel accommodation at 4s. 6d. per night. The bare necessities are provided and it is recommended only for the young and those with experience of observatories on the mainland. Write to the Hon. Secretary, J. L. F. Parslow, Winterslow Cottage, Lincombe Lane, Boar's Hill, Oxford.

Derbyshire

DOVEDALE   OS 111
Dovedale lies in the limestone district north of Ashbourne and is a deep valley cut into the 1,000 foot plateau. The beautiful stream is bordered by natural or semi-natural ash woods. The usual upland valley bird population includes a host of warblers and chats.

SUMMER: dipper, wheatear, redstart, tree pipit, wood and other warblers.

Leave Ashbourne northwards on the A515 and turn left to Dovedale after 1 mile. There is a car park and access is by foot-paths northwards. A large part of Dovedale belongs to the National Trust. Watchers should continue past Dovedale to Milldale, Beresford Dale and Wolfscote Dale all of which hold interest.

GOYT VALLEY   OS 111
The valley lies north-west of Buxton. The river has its origins in Goyt's Moss and falls 1,000 feet in 4–5 miles to Taxal, south of Whaley Bridge. A walk down the valley, or a drive, gives a succession of habitats from gritstone moorland through deciduous woodlands to farmland. Fernilee Reservoir is over

1 mile long and a further reservoir is in process of construction to the south.

SUMMER: curlew, golden plover, red and black grouse, ring ouzel, grey wagtail, dipper, kingfisher, redstart, whinchat, wheatear, warblers, tree pipit.

Leave Buxton westwards on the A53. Fork right on to the A54 and then right again on to A537. Immediately turn right and in a quarter of a mile right once more. Turn left on to Goyt's Moss. This sounds difficult but is straightforward with the OS. Walk (or drive) down to Goyt's Bridge and take the footpath along the edge of the reservoir, down through the woodland to Taxal. The surrounding land is private.

THE TRENT AND NEWTON SOLNEY　　　　　OS 120

The meandering River Trent is joined by the equally meandering and ox-bowed Dove just north of Newton Solney. The wet pasture is usually flooded soon after Christmas and the area then becomes one of the major haunts of wildfowl in the county. There are a few geese most winters and both wild swans are annual in small numbers.

WINTER: wigeon, teal, tufted duck, goosander, goldeneye, pintail, smew, geese, whooper and Bewick's swans, snipe, jack snipe, dunlin.

Leave the A38 between Derby and Burton upon Trent at its junction with the B5008. Continue through Willington and stop near the River Trent. Walk along the southern bank up stream to Newton Solney. Many fishermen on Sundays.

Devonshire

AXE ESTUARY　　　　　　　　OS 176; HT +0:25 Dartmouth

Roughly half-way between Sidmouth and Lyme Regis on the south Devon coast, the Axe is a tiny estuary a mile long and a quarter of a mile wide. Winter wildfowl and waders are never numerous but autumn brings both godwits, ruff and spotted redshank (both occasional in winter). There is, however, always the possibility of rarities at this site, spoonbill and little egret have occurred on several occasions.

WINTER: wigeon, teal, golden plover, dunlin.

SPRING: waders.

AUTUMN: green, wood and common sandpipers, godwits, ruff, spotted redshank, rarities.

Leave the A35 5 miles west of Lyme Regis southwards on the B3172 to Axmouth. View from the road south of the village all the way to the bridge at the mouth.

DARTMOOR NATIONAL PARK   OS 175 and 187

Dartmoor Forest covers an area of over 50,000 acres. It is surrounded by a ring of common land that is known as the Commons of Devon, covering another 50,000 acres. The Dartmoor National Park includes all of this plus another area at least equally large making a grand total of 233,600 acres. Yet, in spite of its vastness, the habitats that it offers are limited, and a visitor can cover them all quite quickly if he so wishes. A great deal of the moor can be seen and explored by car but the advantage lies with those who are willing to do a certain amount of foot slogging. This should not, however, be undertaken lightly. The moor is notorious for its fogs and any inexperienced mountain walker should seek the companionship of an expert before venturing off the metalled roads.

The habitats of Dartmoor are as follows:

1. The open moor with heather, ling, etc., dominant, interrupted by the high Tors with their granite caps.
2. The high level 1,000 feet plus pedunculate oak woods at Wistman's Wood and Piles's Copse at Black Tor Beare.
3. The swift running streams in the wooded valleys.
4. The Forestry Commission's often quite extensive coniferous plantations.
5. The reservoirs.
6. The surrounding rolling countryside with wooded valleys.

On the open heath red grouse, curlew and wheatear are the most interesting birds. Lower heaths hold stonechats and whinchats in appropriate places. The high level oak woods are mere remnants with sparse bird life. The streams are an important focus for all of Dartmoor's birds. High up they are used by ring ouzel, then lower by dipper and grey wagtail.

The Forestry Commission's plantations, especially those round Burrator and Fernworthy Reservoirs, at Soussons Down and Bellever, are good. The bird population varies greatly according to the stage of development of the woods, being most interesting when they are at little more than head height, when a mixture of heath and woodland birds can be found. The reservoirs at Burrator and Fernworthy hold a few wildfowl in winter, and, surrounded by pine woods, they make a pleasant setting for summer bird-watching.

The surrounding countryside, especially along the swift flowing rivers, is extremely beautiful and attractive to many species. Woodland holds both redstart and wood warbler, as well as forming possibly the most densely occupied buzzard area in Britain.

SUMMER: buzzard, raven, red grouse, curlew, wheatear, ring

ouzel, whinchat, stonechat, redstart, grey wagtail, dipper.

One is free to roam over a huge area of the central section, i.e.
Dartmoor Forest proper, though some 30,000 acres mainly in
the north-west are used for military training. Ranges are indi-
cated by notice boards and white posts with two red bands.
They must not be entered when red flags are flying from pro-
minent positions, and firing times can be obtained from local
Post Offices and Police Stations.

In the north leave Okehampton on the A30 westwards and
park after 1½ miles near Fowley. Explore the woods along the
West Okement River and follow that stream uphill to the
high level oakwood at Black Tor Beare. Bear left across open
ground to High Willhays for red grouse and continue northwards to Yes Tor and then to West Mill Tor. Strike northwards to pass Okehampton Camp to metalled road across
railway. Turn left and walk on the southern side of the river
back to original bridge near Fowley.

This hard walk should not be undertaken other than by ex-
perts and then in good weather when the military ranges are
clear.

For the Two Bridges area: (a) Walk northwards up the West
Dart River 1½ miles to Wistman's Wood. Venturing any further
along this valley involves entering the military area. (b) Leave
Two Bridges northwards on the B3212 after 2 miles pass the
pine plantations on the right. At the end of these turn right
to Bellever where there is a Youth Hostel and explore, especially southwards along the East Dart River.

The A362 that leaves the A30 at Whiddon Down, 8 miles
east of Okehampton, and runs south-eastwards to Moreton-
hampstead is the best way of starting for the Fernworthy
Reservoir area. Leave the A362 westwards to Chagford and
follow a maze of lanes up to the southern side of Fernworthy.

Dartmeet lies on the A384 between Two Bridges and Ash-
burton and is a delightful spot and really only the beginning
of the valley oakwoods that stretch almost unbroken downstream to Buckfastleigh. There are walks through the woodland which is National Trust property from Holne.

For Burrator Reservoir leave the A386 at Yelverton on to
the B3212 and take the third on the right outside the town to
Burrator.

EXE ESTUARY   OS 176; HT +0:25 Dartmouth
The tidal stretch of the River Exe between Exeter and
Exmouth is over a mile wide for most of its 5 mile length, pro-
viding several square miles of mud flats at low tide. The inter-

tidal area extends to the stone of the railway embankments that line both shores. Since 1934 the western half has been a sanctuary, now known as the Exe Estuary Bird Sanctuary, extending over 1,000 acres.

The fresh marshes at Exminster hold wildfowl, including a few white-fronted geese most years. The lower estuary holds most interest, with duck dominant, though a flock of 100 dark-bellied brent geese regularly associates with them. A large variety of other species is noted and black-necked and Slavonian grebes are present.

Waders are plentiful at all seasons with a winter population including both godwits, spotted redshank, greenshank, and a few purple sandpipes at Exmouth, and about a hundred sanderling on Dawlish Warren.

Waders and terns are often numerous in autumn and occasional skuas are noted.

WINTER: brent goose, wigeon, pintail, shoveler, merganser, shelduck, goldeneye, eider, scoter, godwits, turnstone, grey plover, ruff, spotted redshank, greenshank, avocet, Slavonian and black-necked grebes.

SPRING: waders, terns.

AUTUMN: godwits, turnstone, ringed plover, whimbrel, common, green and wood sandpipers, greenshank, little stint, curlew, sandpiper, tern, skuas.

Leave Exeter, or avoid it by taking the A38 round its eastern side, and turn left on to the A379. Turn left to Powderham, and at the church there is a very wet tunnel under the railway which gives views of the foreshore. A gate on the left leads to a level crossing (footpath) over the railway and on to the sea wall.

Further south, at Starcross, park off the main road and look for signs 'To Pier and Exmouth Ferry' in the centre of the village next to the Courtney Arms Hotel. Cross the railway, and walk to the end of the pier for excellent views in all directions.

Further south still, follow signs to Dawlish Warren and park in car park. Continue on foot across the Warren and out on to the sand spit for views up the estuary and out to sea.

Views on the eastern bank can be had by leaving Exeter eastward on the A35 and turning right at Clyst St. Mary on to the A377. Take unclassified roads signposted Lympstone. Turn westwards under the railway and view estuary at several points and from the promenade.

LUNDY FIELD STATION AND BIRD OBSERVATORY
OS 163

Lundy Island lies in the Bristol Channel 11 miles north of Hartland Point. It is 3 miles by half a mile and is surrounded by granite cliffs rising to 450 feet. The top is mostly grass and heathland apart from the cultivated area in the south-east, and Millcombe which contains trees and shrubs. In spite of the blanketing effect of large land masses to north and south, the island receives an interesting collection of migrants, including a fair number of rarities.

SPRING: ring ouzel, corncrake, warblers, chats.

SUMMER: Manx shearwater, guillemot, razorbill, puffin, fulmar, kittiwake, raven, buzzard.

AUTUMN: migrants, short-eared owl, Lapland bunting, warblers, chats, flycatchers.

Visitors to the observatory must be members of the Lundy Field Society and pay 5s. 0d. per night for hostel-type accommodation, all inquiries to the Accommodation Officer, A. J. Vickery, 4 Taw View, Bishops Tawton, Barnstaple. Bookings for the hotel or one of the cottages must be made through the Resident Agent, Manor Farm Hotel, Lundy, Bristol Channel, via Bideford, Devon. Access is by MV *Lundy Gannet*, Mr. A. Bealey, Tadworthy, Northam, Bideford (50s. return); or during the summer season by Campbell's Steamer from Ilfracombe (45s. return).

SLAPTON LEY
OS 188

Slapton Ley lies on the south Devon coast 5 miles south of Dartmouth and is part of a private nature reserve and the site of a bird observatory and field centre. The Ley itself stretches for 2½ miles from north to south and is divided into Higher and Lower Leys. The former is almost completely overgrown by reed, while the Lower Ley is open water and a major haunt of winter wildfowl. Both are separated from the sea by the 50 yards of Slapton Sands along which runs the A379. The back slope of this shingle bar is in part overgrown with black thorn and other bushes which provide cover for a host of migrants including very respectable numbers of rarities for a mainland area. Such rarities are mainly biased towards marsh species but have included some bluethroats. The adjacent part of Start Bay is frequented by sea birds at all seasons. In winter numbers of sea duck include parties of eider, while the area is one of the best in the county for divers.

Slapton is a magnificent place and the variety of its habitats ensure first class bird watching at all seasons.

WINTER: tufted duck, pochard, goosander, gadwall, eider, divers, buzzard, raven.

SPRING: terns, waders, passerine migrants.

SUMMER: duck, sedge and reed warblers, buzzard.

AUTUMN: terns, gulls, waders, passerine migrants including rarities.

The A379 between Darthmouth and Kingsbridge provides some of the finest bird watching 'from the road' in the country.

The Ley area is a nature reserve covering 430 acres, under the strict control of Slapton Ley Field Centre, from whom permits can be obtained. The Centre offers a variety of courses including courses on birds. Groups or individuals can follow their own programmes of field activities. An observation cabin is operated on a part time basis by the Devon Bird Watching and Preservation Society and provides accommodation for four residents at a time.

TAMAR ESTUARY

OS 186 and 187; HT +0:16 Plymouth

The Tamar estuary is the large river system that enters the sea at Plymouth excluding the Plym Estuary. In the north the Tamar and Tavy estuaries can be worked from the peninsula between

Tamar-Tavy-Plym: showing main access points to an area that holds several interesting species in winter. Notable are the avocets of Cargreen-Weirquay

the two, while the southern pair includes St. John's Lake and the Lynher River which are worked from the peninsula that ends in Torpoint. The two areas have roughly comparable number of wildfowl though the Tavy–Tamar sometimes holds 20–30 white-fronted geese, and their favourite resort at Weirquay is also a good vantage point for the famous avocets that regularly winter. The freshwater reservoir at Lopwell (40 acres) is worth a look for duck. The waders include wintering black-tailed godwit (150) usually on the Tavy.

WINTER: wigeon, teal, black-tailed godwit, avocet, turnstone, oystercatcher.

AUTUMN: whimbrel, turnstone, spotted redshank, bar-tailed and black-tailed godwits, greenshank.

1. NORTHERN GROUP: Leave Tavistock westwards on the A390 and turn left on to unclassified roads after 2 miles, signposted Bere Alston. Watch for further signposts for Bere Ferrers. To view from the southern shore, leave the A386 westwards north of Crownhill on to a maze of narrow lanes signposted Maristow. Watch out for signpost to Horsham on left. Turn down narrow lane later becoming a rough track to the estuary.

For the Tamar follow signposts from either Bere Ferrers or Bere Alston to Weirquay, but you will probably have to ask the way. If the whole object of the trip is to see avocets, it is best to pay the toll (2s. 0d. per car) across the Tamar Bridge to Saltash. Leave on the A374 but watch for A388 on outskirts, and turn off at Carkeel to Botus Fleming, where turn right to Cargreen. View from quay at half tide.

2. SOUTHERN GROUP: Leave Plymouth on the Torpoint Ferry. At Torpoint turn left along Marine Drive, right at the end and then first left to the road overlooking St. John's Lake.

Continue westwards on the A38 and stop soon after Antony where views of the large area of the Lynher can be had beside the road.

TORRIDGE–TAW ESTUARY
                              OS 163; HT −0:17 Milford Haven
The two rivers enter the sea at the centre of Barnstaple Bay on the north Devon coast. The Taw estuary is the largest, stretching 8 miles inland to Barnstaple, while the Torridge stretches 4 miles southwards to, and beyond, Bideford. At their confluence both estuaries are protected from the sea by large dune systems with the famous Braunton Burrows to the north, and Northam Burrows on the southern side. The former are partly a National Nature Reserve and partly a military training zone. Both systems provide excellent vantage points for

viewing the estuary as most birds congregate at the confluence. Wildfowl in particular use this area and flight on to Braunton Marshes to feed. White-fronts are irregular in small numbers.

Waders are most numerous in autumn, though sanderling often winter on Northam Burrows, from where quite interesting numbers of seabirds can be seen in autumn.

WINTER: wigeon, teal, shelduck, grey and golden plover, turnstone, bar-tailed godwit, sanderling.

AUTUMN: bar-tailed godwit, whimbrel, greenshank, kittiwake, common tern.

Leave Barnstaple westwards on the A361 to Braunton, turn left in the town centre and continue on B3231 towards Saunton. Take the second left and continue to the estuary along the back of Braunton Burrows. Walk right out to Crow Point.

From the south, views can be obtained from Appledore Quay, and Broads and a track lead out to Northam Burrows.

WARNING: keep well clear of Braunton Burrows when the red flag is flying indicating military training.

Dorset

ABBOTSBURY SWANNERY   OS 178
Situated at the western end of Chesil Fleet, the Swannery itself dates back to at least the fourteenth century, since when the swans have been protected by the landowners. Recent growth of the number of birds has caused a limit of eight hundred to be introduced, which is thought to be about the optimum.

SUMMER: mute swan, common and little terns, ringed plover.

Leave the A35 southwards at the western end of Martingtown, 3 miles west of Dorchester. Follow signposts to Abbotsbury. Take the southward turning to the Swannery, half a mile away. Entrance fee is 2s. 6d., less for children, and one can then walk around the pens, the botanical gardens and along the beach as far as the Dragon's Teeth.

ARNE HEATH   OS 179
The extensive heathland that once covered such a vast area of Dorset has been disappearing at an alarming rate. Thus National Nature Reserves have been established at Studland and Hartland, and in 1966 the RSPB established its Arne Heath Reserve covering 700 acres. Arne lies on a peninsula jutting into Poole Harbour from the south and is mainly covered with heather and gorse, though there are some stands of Scots pine. The most important species is the Dartford warbler, at present

at a very low ebb, and doubtless the Society hopes that what
it has already done for the bearded tit it can repeat for this
elusive warbler.

WINTER: wildfowl, waders.

SUMMER: Dartford warbler, nightjar, stonechat.

Access is by permit available in advance from the RSPB.

BROWNSEA ISLAND   OS 179; HT at Poole

Brownsea is the largest island in Poole Harbour 1½ miles long
by three-quarters of a mile wide. Its 500 acres include heath,
woodland, lake and marsh. It is owned by the National Trust
who have leased the northern half to the Dorset NT as a
nature reserve. About 180 species have been identified on
Brownsea since 1962, about 50 of which breed. It is the lagoon
and marsh area that provide the most interesting bird-watching. At passage periods the lagoon holds large numbers of
waders, especially at high tide when it forms one of the
major roosts for the Harbour. Winter population of waders
includes good numbers of both godwits, a few green sandpipers, and occasional avocet.

WINTER: wigeon, shellduck, pintail, godwits, grey plover,
turnstone, green sandpiper, spotted redshank, avocet.

SUMMER: terns, nightjar, heron, woodcock, sedge warbler.

AUTUMN: wood sandpiper, whimbrel, greenshank, godwits.

Access is by boat from Sandbanks Ferry (2s. 6d.) and Poole
Quay (3s. 0d.) to the quay on the Island. Private boats may
land on the south shore (excluding the Castle Beach) and at
the western end of the island only. Boats are also available,
though less regularly, from Shell Bay and Rockley Sands.
There is a landing fee of 2s. 6d. Access to the reserve is
restricted to guided tours starting near the church on Wednesdays, Thursdays and Saturdays, at 11.15 a.m. and 2.45 p.m.
The charge is 5s. 0d., or 2s. 6d. for members of the National
Trust or Dorset NT. There is a public hide near the quay
equipped with a telescope. Children are half price.

POOLE HARBOUR   OS 179; HT at Poole

The Harbour is a huge natural inlet lying immediately west of
the Bournemouth–Poole conurbation. It is much used by the
public as a holiday ground for sailing and more recently,
water skiing. This has reduced its attractiveness as a breeding
area and to a lesser extent, to passage migrants, though the
improvements at Brownsea are some compensation.

Most duck concentrate in the north-eastern part of the Harbour and all three species of divers and all four species of

grebe are regular, with Slavonian and black-necked often quite numerous. These species are often found in Poole, Studland and Shell Bays as well as the Harbour.

In winter black-tailed godwits outnumber bar-tailed and other species include the odd common sandpiper and occasional avocet.

WINTER: wigeon, shelduck, pintail, shoveler, scaup, merganser, goldeneye, smew, divers, black-necked grebe, Slavonian grebe, black-tailed and bar-tailed godwits, turnstone, common sandpiper.

SPRING: waders, terns.

AUTUMN: divers, grebes, wildfowl, whimbrel, spotted redshank, black-tailed and bar-tailed godwits, greenshank, knot, little stint, sanderling, terns.

Access to this vast area is at several points:

1. At South Haven Point, and along the edge of Brands Bay access via Toll (see Studland Heath) from south.
2. The Shore Road on the north side of the Ferry, the Blue Lagoon and Harbour Yacht Club are all good in winter.
3. Rockley Sands caravan site.

PORTLAND HARBOUR – FERRYBRIDGE   OS 178

Situated south of Weymouth where Chesil Beach joins the Isle of Portland; Ferrybridge refers to the general area at the eastern end of the fleet and includes a small area of inter-tidal sand and mud that regularly attracts small numbers of waders, terns and gulls. It does, however, produce more than its fair share of rarities and unusual species, including little gull, and is best during migration periods.

Portland Harbour is mainly known as a haunt of sea-duck, all three divers and Slavonian grebe.

WINTER: (at Portland Harbour) merganser, eider, scoter, divers, Slavonian grebe.

SPRING AND AUTUMN: (at Ferrybridge) waders, gulls, terns, little gull.

Leave Weymouth southwards on the A354 signposted Portland. Cross the Ferrybridge and park in car park on right overlooking the inter-tidal area. Views of Portland Harbour can be obtained from here by crossing the railway and sitting on the Harbour wall.

See map page 43.

PORTLAND BILL   OS 178

The headquarters of Portland Bird Observatory and Field Centre. By virtue of its geographical postion jutting some 6 miles out into the Channel the area receives large numbers of migrants of all types. Small dry stone-walled fields and thorny hedges hold stock and the odd arable crop. The obelisk at the Bill makes an admirable shelter for the excellent sea-watching and regular species include Manx and Balearic shearwaters.

The commoner chats, warblers and flycatchers pass through in large numbers, and an unusual migrant is the occasional Dartford warbler. Rarities in recent years have included great reed, aquatic, olivaceous, subalpine, Bonelli's and yellow-browed warblers, while melodious and icterine warblers, and tawny pipits are annual.

Almost any other rarity can and does turn up and well over 2,000 birds are ringed annually.

WINTER: wildfowl, auks, divers, grebes, purple sandpiper.

SPRING: scoter, auks, divers, waders, gulls, chats, warblers, flycatchers.

AUTUMN: Manx and Balearic shearwaters, fulmar, gannet, scoter, velvet scoter, kittiwake, little gull, terns, auks, chats, warblers, flycatchers, rarities.

Leave Weymouth southwards following signs to Portland on the A354. The observatory is situated in the Old Light on the left a quarter of a mile before the Bill and the main areas for passerines are the fields on the right of the road.

Portland Bird Observatory and Field Centre is open from 1st March to 31st October and at other times by arrangement with the resident Warden. It is the 'Hilton' of bird observatories. Accommodation is 6s. 0d. per night in six small dormitories and 10s. 0d. per night including an evening meal at peak periods. Bookings must be made in advance.

All correspondence and booking to The Warden, Portland Bird Observatory and Field Centre, Old Lower Light, Portland, Dorset.

RADIPOLE LAKE AND LODMOOR   OS 178

Both lie in Weymouth and are separated by only half a mile of the Melcombe area of the town. Radipole is the estuarine backwater of the River Wey and its water level is artificially controlled. It was declared a sanctuary in 1948 and now consists of a series of inter-connected lagoons and a large reed bed. Lodmoor is a low lying area of rough grazing intersected by dykes and very liable to flooding. The creation of rubbish dumps on the area has reduced its attractiveness though it still holds birds and has a long list of rarities to its credit.

Wildfowl numbers in what is virtually a town park are remarkable, and waders are outstanding at migration times.

Radipole Lake, Lodmoor and Portland Harbour: outstanding urban bird-watching on all sides of Weymouth

Terns are numerous at Radipole with black terns being almost continuously present in autumn. The lake is also one of the most consistent haunts of the little gull in England.

SPRING: waders, terns, garganey.

SUMMER: sedge, reed and grasshopper warblers.

AUTUMN: little ringed plover, sandpipers, spotted redshank, greenshank, little stint, terns, black tern, little gull, rails and crakes.

Lodmoor lies to the north of the coastal A353 out of Weymouth.

For Radipole pass under a small bridge at the north-western end of the boat basin on to a roughly asphalted area for views over lagoons. Continue along path between gorse for passerines and reed beds.

See Map, above.

STUDLAND HEATH   OS 179

The Heath lies on the south side of Poole Harbour, and was
declared a National Nature Reserve in 1962, covering 429 acres.
Though the various heath plants, especially heather, are dominant, the reserve includes dunes, marsh and woodland and the
freshwater lagoon of Little Sea. This wide variety of habitat
leads to a wealth of bird life in a comparatively small area.

The usual heathland birds breed and include Dartford
warblers. The chances of seeing one without being shown by
the Warden are nil. Amongst waders and wildfowl there is a
great deal of coming and going between Little Sea and Poole
Harbour and the population is very similar. Specifically Studland birds are the large flock of sanderling in Studland Bay.

WINTER: wigeon, teal, waders, godwits, sanderling.

SUMMER: Dartford warbler, stonechat, nightingale, redpoll,
warblers.

AUTUMN: sanderling.

Leave Wareham southwards on the A351 towards Swanage.
Turn left after 4 miles at Corfe Castle on to B3351 and continue
to Studland. Pass straight through to the toll gate, a toll of
4s. 0d. is payable to use the road but an additional 1s. 0d. includes the ferry to Sandbanks. About half a mile north of the
toll gate a hill on the right screens Little Sea from view and
a gully has been cut up to the observation hide and headquarters of the reserve. Report to the Warden. This route can
be reversed from Sandbanks on the Poole side.

There is some danger from unexploded missiles.

Essex

ABBERTON RESERVOIR   OS 162

Lies 4 miles south of Colchester, the same distance north of the
Blackwater Estuary, and is England's number one reservoir.
Its 1,240 acres is spread over an area 4 miles by 1 mile, and it
was completed in 1940. Three-quarters of the 12 miles peri-
meter is concrete banked and the depth of water varies down
to 50 feet. Such a huge expanse so near the Essex coast was
bound to attract wildfowl, but the Abberton numbers are
often staggering. The following maxima have been recorded,
usually in October–November: mallard 4,000, teal 12,000,
wigeon 5,000, pintail 450, shoveler 1,300, pochard 3,800,
tufted 600, goldeneye 350, goosander 85, smew 90, mute swan
450. Among the more erratic but nevertheless reasonably regular visitors are Bewick's swan, white-fronted goose, gadwall

and outstandingly red-crested pochard. Birds of this species regularly occur but were labelled 'escapes' until quite recently; the majority are now accepted as wild birds.

Almost any wader is liable to turn up on passage. Many can be found away from the reservoir along the nearby Roman River valley, if it is flooded at the right time. Other passage migrants include good numbers of commic and especially black terns. Almost anything can turn up here.

WINTER: wigeon, pintail, shoveler, pochard, tufted duck, goldeneye, goosander, smew, Bewick's swan, white-fronted goose, gadwall, red-crested pochard, scaup, grebes, divers.

SPRING: whimbrel, black tern, garganey.

AUTUMN: red-crested pochard, garganey, greenshank, ruff, common, Arctic and black terns, hirundines.

Access to the reservoir banks and surrounds is restricted to a number of officers of the Essex Bird Watching and Preservation Society. Members of this Society can usually gain access by arranging a visit with the Society's Chairman or Secretary.

Quite large areas of the reservoir can be seen from roads and a great many bird-watchers never bother to enter. Leave Colchester southwards on the B1026. After 5 miles, an iron gate on the left, set back from the road, gives views over a quite large area. A further three-quarters of a mile south is the main bird-watching causeway. Continue southwards and after 1 mile the B1026 turns sharply left; at this point an unclassified road leads northwards signposted Layer Breton. In half a mile this leads to another causeway across the stretch with natural banks.

BRADWELL BIRD OBSERVATORY

OS 150; HT —0:20 Sheerness

The Observatory was established in 1954 at the mouth of the River Blackwater on the southern shore near the Dengie Flats area. Bradwell is an idea centre for exploring the estuary and the flats from St. Peters to Holliwell Point.

Waders are numerous and a first class variety is noted in autumn, good numbers are caught and ringed. Other species include snow bunting and twite and brent geese in winter.

Spring and autumn bring numbers of passerine migrants, including the regular chats, warblers and flycatchers, and larger numbers of thrushes and goldcrests.

WINTER: brent goose, grey plover, turnstone, snowbunting, twite.

SPRING: waders, migrants.

SUMMER: oystercatcher, black-headed gull.

AUTUMN: grey plover, turnstone, whimbrel, sanderling, curlew sandpiper, little stint, goldcrest, snow bunting, twite, thrushes.

Leave the A127 at Nevendon northwards on to the A132. In 2 miles pass through Wickford and continue to A130. Cross this on to B1012 and continue on B1010, B1020 to Southminster. Then B1021 to Bradwell on Sea. British Railways run to Southminster, continue by bus to Bradwell.

Spartan accommodation provided at the Observatory 3s. 6d. to 5s. 0d. per night. Write to A. B. Old, Bata Hotel, East Tilbury, Essex.

DENGIE FLATS   OS 162; HT −0:41 Sheerness

Between the Rivers Blackwater and Crouch lies a huge expanse of rough grazing, intersected by an intricate maze of dykes and streams. Between Bradwell and Burnham stretch 16 miles of sea wall making one of the most daunting birdwatching walks in the country. The area is wonderful for wildfowl with dabbling duck especially numerous. Wigeon (3,000+) and brent geese (2,000) are dominant and this area with Foulness and the Blackwater forms the headquarters of the latter species in Britain; they belong almost exclusively to the black-bellied form (*Branta bernicla bernicla*).

Waders are numerous on the fields and mud flats and hen harrier and short-eared owl are frequent in winter. High tide visits are essential.

WINTER: brent goose, wigeon, teal, shelduck, golden plover, knot, curlew, grey plover, hen harrier, short-eared owl.

SPRING AND AUTUMN: waders.

For route to the area, see Bradwell. Access is awkward and is probably best achieved from Eastlands Farm at Bradwell, then south along the sea wall to Sandbeach outfall, returning over the fresh marshes via Glebe Farm.

Alternatively, leave Burnham eastwards before the Station and follow the metalled road to East Wick. Continue through Coney Hall to the sea wall at the mouth of the Crouch: walk eastwards to Holliwell Point and beyond.

For the really hardy, with warm and waterproof clothing and sustenance; arrive Bradwell and walk all round to Burnham on Crouch – 16 miles of sea wall.

HANNINGFIELD RESERVOIR   OS 161

Situated 6 miles south of Chelmsford and though overshadowed by the more famous Abberton, is ranked sixth among England's top wildfowl reservoirs. Completed in 1954, it covers 870 acres and is further from the coast than Abberton. There are large numbers of wildfowl in winter and both gadwall and garganey are present in spring and autumn and often breed.

In autumn there is a build up of little grebes (300) and black-necked grebes are regular.

Waders of a great variety are present on passage, when almost every visit produces something of interest. Terns, including occasional Arctic, breed and black and commic are present in autumn.

WINTER: teal, wigeon, shoveler, pochard, tufted duck, goldeneye, smew, divers, grebes, dunlin.

SPRING: waders, black tern, garganey.

SUMMER: terns, garganey.

AUTUMN: little ringed plover, whimbrel, wood, green and common sandpipers, spotted redshank, greenshank, little stint, curlew sandpiper, ruff, commic tern, black tern, garganey.

Permits to enter are available only to members of the Essex Bird Watching and Preservation Society and can be obtained from one of several officers. Members should contact the Secretary.

Good views of the reservoir can be obtained from public roads. Leave Chelmsford southwards on the A130. After some 6½ miles turn left, signposted West Hanningfield, turn left in the village and view in 2–300 yards at the end of the dam where a hill drops down southward. Continue southwards but watch out for a pool on the left for passage waders. Bear right and view on right, and again half a mile further opposite entrance to the Hall. Continue taking right hand turns at two T-junctions to near Whitelilies Farm, where quite close views can be obtained.

WALTON ON THE NAZE

OS 150; HT −0:09 Harwich

Situated on the coast immediately north of the resorts of Clacton and Frinton. The area that concerns the bird-watcher is the Naze to the north of the town, the saltings out to Stone Point, and the huge tidal complex of Hamford Water.

The Naze is well positioned to receive migrants and the bushes along the cliff path are always worth searching. Waders and wildfowl are the specialities with brent geese and various sea duck outstanding. Horsey Island holds a flock of feral greylag geese. The only purple sandpipers on this coast frequent the broken sea wall, twite and snow bunting are winter visitors to Stone Point, and sea watching for skuas can be lucrative.

WINTER: brent goose, scoter, merganser, goldeneye, shelduck, eider, curlew, grey plover, bar-tailed godwit, purple sandpiper, snow bunting, twite, short-eared owl.

SUMMER: black-headed gull, common and little tern.

AUTUMN: grey plover, godwits, green sandpiper, greenshank, curlew sandpipers, skuas, chats, warblers.

Walton on the Naze: the route out to Stone Point involves crossing channels that fill up at high tide. The return route should be exactly the outward route back to the mainland, but then westwards to Walton Channel

Follow the main roads to Clacton, but leave the A133 at Weeley on to the B1033. This runs to Frinton and then becomes the B1336 to Walton. Follow the main street northwards and park near the cliff edge. Follow the cliff footpath. Watch for purple sandpipers on the broken sea wall, and twite and waders on the marshes. Cross the tidal creeks at low tide (making sure of your return) out to Stone Point.

Leave Walton on the B1034 to Kirby le Soken but turn right in 1½ miles to Kirby Cross.

Gloucestershire

FOREST OF DEAN   OS 142 and 156

A National Forest Park covering some 25,000 acres. The area
has been forested since time immemorial and the birds repre-
sent as complete a hardwood woodland community as can be
found in any part of the British Isles. The whole area, 8 miles
by 6 miles, is worthy of exploration, though the area in the
south-west is the most attractive.

Notable is a large population of pied flycatchers which are
not generally viewable by the public. More widespread are the
usual woodland warblers and amongst the specialities are
sparrowhawk, buzzard, red-backed shrike and woodlark.

The woodland streams attract a large population, the area
around Parkend is very good and is favoured by Crossbills
during irruptions.

SUMMER: buzzard, sparrowhawk, nightjar, red-backed
shrike, dipper, raven, wood and grasshopper warblers, pied
flycatcher, redstart, woodlark, siskin, hawfinch.

The Forest lies between the rivers Severn and Wye, and between the A4136 to Monmouth and the A48 to Chepstow.
Access is generally unrestricted with the exception of the pied
flycatcher experiment which is being undertaken by the
Forestry Commission, from whom permission must be obtained to view.

The Parkend area is best reached from the A48. Turn north
at Lydney on the B4234, NOT the B4231. After 4 miles turn left
on the B4431 and explore the area to the south.

Local newsagents sell guide books to the area, of which the
Wye Dean Tourist Guide is the best. Various pamphlets showing the Ramblers' Association waymarked paths are also available.

Several local inns provide bed and breakfast and there is the
Forestry Commission's Christchurch camping site.

THE NEW GROUNDS, SLIMBRIDGE   OS 156

The New Grounds lie on the south-east bank of the Severn and
extend for some 3 miles north-east of the Severn Railway
Bridge. The 1,000 acres of enclosed pasture and high salt
marsh plus the huge area of sand-flats is managed as a wildfowl refuge by the Wildfowl Trust.

The Trust, formerly the Severn Wildfowl Trust, was established by Peter Scott in 1946 close to the refuge and to the
Berkeley New Decoy, which was built in 1843. A large series

of ponds has been excavated and numerous enclosures house the best and largest collection of wildfowl in the world. A unique contribution to conservation was made at Slimbridge with the building up of a captive flock of Néné or Hawaiian geese that held over half of the world's population of this all but extinct species before a number of birds were sent to Hawaii and released. As a safety measure against endemic disease, a separate collection has been set up at Peakirk in Northamptonshire.

The Trust not only manages these two collections, which are both open to visitors, but it is leading the way in wildfowl conservation in a realistic alliance with the Wildfowlers' Association of Great Britain and Ireland, and has a number of research workers actively engaged on the scientific study of wildfowl. It has carried out the large-scale ringing of ducks and geese in its two decoys, by means of rocket-netting and on expeditions to the Arctic breeding grounds. The ringing of swans has been encouraged by the Trust and perhaps as many as one in four mute swans in the country now carries a ring.

The Trust's grounds prove attractive to a huge range of birds, especially duck, which fly in from the estuary to feed. The white-fronted geese on the Dumbles usually build up to 1,000 by Christmas and may number 4,000–5,000 in the new year. All other species of British geese have occurred here, including lesser white-front in most years. A flock of over a hundred Bewick's swans winter here, spending part of each day in one of the enclosures. Observation hides have been constructed along the sea wall overlooking the Dumbles to which parties of members are escorted at 1130, 1400 and 1500 hours in winter for a close view of the wild geese. There is also a hide accessible to all visitors overlooking the pond in the Rushy Pen frequented by the wild Bewick's swans.

Waders, too, benefit from the lack of disturbance and on both passages there are good collections of birds. Collared doves are regularly present, being attracted by the free grain; and peregrines are seen most winters.

RESIDENT: waterfowl collection, collared dove.

WINTER: white-fronted goose, Bewick's swan, wigeon, shoveler, pintail, gadwall, waders, peregrine.

SPRING AND AUTUMN: grey plover, whimbril, godwits, green and wood sandpipers, spotted redshank, greenshank, little stint, ruff, turnstone.

Leave the A38 threequarters of a mile south of Cambridge signposted Slimbridge and follow signs to Wildfowl Trust. Admission is daily from 9.30, times of closing varying according to season. Members only are admitted up to 12 noon on Sundays, and they may take a guest without charge. Parties of members are escorted to the Trusts' observation hides. Meals and refreshments are obtainable in the restaurant in the Trusts' grounds.

WYE VALLEY   OS Tourist Map Wye Valley
The Wye runs in a beautiful wooded valley forming the boundary between Gloucestershire and Monmouthshire. The woods are interrupted here and there by steep limestone outcrops producing a dramatic effect. There is a good variety of breeding birds.

SUMMER: dipper, grey wagtail, raven, buzzard, warblers.

The best arrangement is to park at one bridge, walk to the next, cross and walk back. There are bridges at Bigsweir, west of St. Briavels, at Brockweir, near Tintern, at Chapel Hill (foot only) and Chepstow.

Hampshire

CHRISTCHURCH HARBOUR
                    OS 179; HT −0:17 Poole Bridge
This is the first area of open foreshore east of Bournemouth. The Harbour, though comparatively small, has quite large mudbanks with areas of saltings and shingle, but is disturbed by sailing in summer. Stanpit Marsh is a local nature reserve of Christchurch Borough Council, covering 112 acres. It consists of saltings, tidal mud, fresh pools, reed beds and water meadows. In autumn all of the usual waders are present in small numbers and the gorse bushes sometimes hold interesting passerine migrants. Better for these species is Hengistbury Head on the southern side of the Harbour which has been the headquarters of the Christchurch Harbour Ringing Group since 1956. Sea bird movements can be good.

WINTER: dunlin, divers and grebes, scoter.

AUTUMN: little stint, curlew sandpiper, sanderling, skuas, auks, terns, yellow wagtail, sedge and reed warblers, passerine migrants.

There is a public path on the east side of Town Bridge over the River Avon to Stanpit.

No Ringing in the area before contacting Mr. K. T. Standring, 74 Somerford Road, Christchurch.

Beach chalets are available at the Mudeford end of Hengistbury from the Christchurch Corporation, but these must be booked well in advance.

THE GINS AND NEEDS OAR POINT
OS 180 and New Forest Tourist Map

At the mouth of the Beaulieu River on the western bank, the area consists principally of a shingle bank stretching out into the mouth of the river, an older shingle bank with grass and scrub, a tidal creek between the two, and a series of shallow pools protected by the seawall. There is additionally the low mud-covered Bull Island, that can be reached at low tide.

The whole area is justly famous for the numbers of waders that it attracts, notably spotted redshank, for whom the area is the main haunt in Britain.

WINTER: wigeon, shoveler, spotted redshank, greenshank, black-tailed godwit, golden plover, turnstone.

SPRING: bar-tailed godwit, spotted redshank.

SUMMER: black-headed gull, Sandwich and common terns.

AUTUMN: spotted redshank, greenshank, black-tailed godwit.

Leave the main A35 on the northern side of Lyndhurst between Bournemouth and Southampton, and take the B3056 southward to Beaulieu. Turn right in the village on to the B3054 and then left in a quarter of a mile on to a minor road towards Bucklers Hard. Keep left after 600 yards and right after 1 mile. Turn left down the edge of a copse after turning sharp right at St. Leonards. Follow this past the farm towards the shore and park where a track leads off to the left towards Needs Oar Point.

Access is by permit only and the area is well wardened by the Hampshire and Isle of Wight Naturalists' Trust.

LANGSTONE HARBOUR AND FARLINGTON
MARSHES   OS 181; HT +0:06 Portsmouth

Langstone Harbour is a vast area of inter-tidal mud and salting. Winter brings hordes of wildfowl and waders with the flock of brent geese (up to 900) being the largest on the south coast. They may be seen from Hayling Island at high tide or from Farlington at other times. The flock of up to 30 black-necked grebes is especially important.

Waders are very numerous and form an almost solid mass of birds on the high tide roosts on Baker's and South Binness Islands. Dunlin reach 15,000 in the Harbour and there is also a large roost of this species on Portsmouth Airfield. Greenshank usually winter in very small numbers and black-tailed outnumber bar-tailed godwits. Passage is more important at Farlington Marshes, where an area of fresh marsh extends into the Harbour for a mile from the northern shore.

The area of grazing is drained by a stream which ends in a

muddy reed-fringed lagoon where some of the rarest waders have been noted. The thorn bush area in the north is worth a look for passerine migrants at appropriate seasons.

The concentration of gulls at Eastney sewage outfall regularly includes extreme rarities and held an Iceland gull, 2 Mediterranean gulls, a little gull and a Sabine's gull in one recent year.

WINTER: brent goose, wigeon, teal, shelduck, merganser, goldeneye, long-tailed duck, bar-tailed and black-tailed godwits, grey plover, oystercatcher, greenshank, knot, sanderling, divers, grebes, black-necked grebe, short-eared owl.
SPRING: godwits, whimbrel, sandpipers, garganey.
SUMMER: grey plover, bar-tailed godwit, terns.
AUTUMN: grey plover, whimbrel, green, wood and common sandpipers, greenshank, little stint, spotted redshank, godwits, ruff, short-eared owl, passerines.

1. Farlington Marsh is a nature reserve of the Hampshire and Isle of Wight NT and is of free access. See map. At low tide and with gumboots one can walk out over North Binness and Long Island for a period of six hours to obtain excellent views over the main channel.

Langstone Harbour and Farlington Marshes: a standard route leaves the car park, turns southward to the southern tip of the Marshes for views of Langstone Harbour, and returns via the eastern shore and the bushes area to the north

2. Leave the A27 at Havant southwards on to Hayling Island. Continue to South Hayling and turn right into Station Road, pass the station, follow on to Park Road and then turn right into North Shore Road. A fence at the end is navigable at the left end on to a path running along the Harbour wall.

3. The Harbour mouth can be reached on either side and there is a ferry from Portsea to Hayling for walkers. Do not neglect Eastney sewage outfall.

NEW FOREST   OS Tourist Map New Forest

The Forest lies between Southampton Water and the Hampshire Avon and is not, as is commonly thought, the result of William the Conqueror removing farmers to make a hunting ground. The Royal Forest covers 64,707 acres, of which 2,000 acres are permanently enclosed and private, and 16,000 acres which are free of common rights as long as they remain enclosed. There remain some 45,000 acres of permanent common, of which 5,000 acres is woodland. There is an additional area of 6,000 acres abutting on to the Forest provided by a ring of 22 other commons, making a grand total of 51,000 acres of commonland.

The underlying rocks are basically sandy and give rise to heather scenery with occasional large areas of gorse, bracken, scrub and rough grass. The woodlands are mainly mixed and vary enormously in age. Quite large areas of old oak and beech forest exist, while more recent plantings include areas of Scots pine.

A wonderful range of breeding birds includes crossbills, a few pairs of siskin and a small colony of firecrests. The Forest is the stronghold of the Dartford warbler in Britain but numbers are at present very low and the birds are hard to find in 144 square miles.

It has been said that the New Forest is generally a disappointment birdwise, but though a day trip can miss all the specialities, one needs only a fair amount of luck and persistency for a truly wonderful day, week, or month.

SUMMER: woodcock, wood warbler, nightingale, goldcrest, redstart, crossbill, redpoll, hawfinch, grey wagtail, hobby, sparrow hawk, buzzard, stonechat, nightjar, Dartford warbler, red-backed shrike, woodlark, curlew, redshank, snipe, wheatear.

The whole of the Forest area merits attention and, in particular, the status of the Dartford warbler and red-backed shrike is under constant inquiry. There are three Forest

Nature Reserves where access is restricted to the trackways and rides; at Bramshaw (525 acres), Mark Ash (226 acres) and Matley and Denny (2,577 acres).

If there is no time to explore and find areas of your own the following are worth a visit – but there are many other good spots:

1. Drive from Brockenhurst across Rhinefield to enter the varied but huge woodland area near Rhinefield Lodge. Continue on the A35 and cross directly into the Knightwood Oak area, through Mark Ash and out on to the A31.

2. Of the heaths, Beaulieu is amongst the best. The northern half west of the B3054 between Beaulieu and Dibden is good; and in the south the area west of Crockford Bridge can be so.

3. The Beaulieu Road area on the Lyndhurst–Beaulieu Road, B3056, especially on the south side next to Denny Wood.

4. The north-western heaths north of the A31 out to Dockens Water and Broomy Inclosure.

At all times be careful of ponies on the road. There are hundreds of accidents every year.

Camping is permitted from mid-March to mid-October but permits must be obtained before setting up camp from the Forestry Commission, Red Lodge, Lyndhurst. Monday–Friday. Camping Offices at Hollands Wood (A337); Queens House Grounds, Lyndhurst (off A35); Marlpit Oak (off B3055); Shave Green, Cadnam (A337); Ashurst (A35) and Stoney Cross Airfield (off A31), issue permits on Friday evenings, Saturdays and Sundays during the season.

NEWTOWN MARSH, ISLE OF WIGHT   OS 180

The marsh was formed when the sea wall was breached by gales in November 1954, 130 acres are now flooded at high tide. This is an excellent area for wildfowl and waders, including a good wintering flock of black-tailed godwits, and the occasional wintering greenshank.

WINTER: teal, wigeon, shelduck, black-tailed godwit, greenshank.

SPRING: waders.

SUMMER: black-headed gull.

AUTUMN: golden and grey plovers, greenshank, little stint, ruff.

Leave the A3054 6 miles west of Newport and turn right to Newtown. In the village turn left and continue as far west as possible, a footpath from here crosses on to the sea wall. For the eastern end of the wall, access is through Town Copse (National Trust).

SELBORNE   OS 169
The village is on the B3006 between Alton and Petersfield. It is celebrated as the home of Gilbert White who wrote its *Natural History* and founded the science of ornithology. The beech hanger to the south is reached by the famous zig-zag path made by the White brothers and tea can be obtained at The Wakes Museum.

SUMMER: wood warbler, warblers, goldcrest.

Leave Alton on the B3006 to Selborne. The Wakes is on the right and the path to the Hanger starts just past the Selborne Arms.

TITCHFIELD HAVEN AND HILL HEAD   OS 180
The area lies on the Solent between Gosport and the Hamble River, and consists of two branches of the River Meon flowing through freshwater marshes. Though there is a public footpath along the lesser stream, the whole area is private and is strictly maintained as a sanctuary. The winter population includes large numbers of wildfowl with black-tailed godwit (500) and the usual waders. Hill Head is an exciting place for a sea watch in autumn, when the usual terns are often joined by roseate. The marshes themselves are excellent at this time and regularly hold a variety of 'fresh' waders with black terns frequently present.

WINTER: wigeon, teal, shoveler, black-tailed godwit, turnstone.

SPRING: black tern, whimbrel.

SUMMER: sedge and reed warblers, roseate and black terns, black-tailed godwit, green and wood sandpipers, ruff, rarities.

Leave the A27 at Titchfield on to the B3334 to Stubbington, turn right to Hill Head. At the shore turn right to the Harbour Bridge. The public footpath up the western stream starts on the western side of the main stream some 150 yards past the bridge. Dr. C. Suffern meets all comers every Saturday and Sunday, except from 25 March to 1 May, at the Bridge at 10.30 a.m. and leads a walk along the eastern (private) side, returning by about 12.30 p.m. He is the only person permitted to do this and thus provides a unique service to his fellow ornithologists. Though no notice need be given, it would be courteous to drop Dr. Suffern a card at Hook Cottage, Hook with Warsash, Hants, noting one's intention to be present. In bad weather he may not be able to come.

The best place for a sea watch is at Meon shore where the public footpath up the Meon begins to the west of Hill Head.

Herefordshire and Radnorshire

LUGG MEADOWS (Hereford)   OS 142

The meadows border the River Lugg to the north-east of Hereford, just before it joins the Wye. They are divided into Upper and Lower Meadows and lie north and south of the A465. In winter the meadows flood and wildfowl are plentiful. A few waders including jack snipe occur most years.

WINTER: wigeon, teal, pintail, shoveler, pochard, waders.

Leave Hereford on the A465 or A438 and stop at Lugg Bridge, there is a path along the river bank.

RADNOR MOORS (Radnor)   OS 141

Radnor Moors lie in the huge area between Kington, Builth Wells and Penybont and rise to 2,000 feet. The area is rather bleak moorland and there is surprisingly little afforestation. Red grouse are widespread and other upland species can be seen.

SUMMER: raven, buzzard, red grouse, wheatear, whinchat, ring ouzel, merlin, dipper, grey wagtail.

The whole area is surrounded by main roads and intersected by numerous minor roads. Perhaps the best is from Kington to Gladestry and then south-westwards via Newchurch, Bryngwyn, Rhosgoch, Llanbedr and Llan Bwchllyn Lake. But exploration is necessary.

WIGMORE (Hereford)   OS 129

On the A4110, 3 miles south of its junction with the A4113 and 8 miles east of Knighton. The area has three main attractions, the Wigmore Rolls, a large area of mainly coniferous forest to the west of the village, the winter floods along the Teme on either side of Criftin Ford Bridge, and the ground north of Wigmore village. The latter holds sizeable flocks of duck, and the woods hold the usual breeding species but are particularly attractive in winter. During irruption years they are a favourite haunt of crossbills.

WINTER: wigeon, teal, siskin, redpoll.
SUMMER: teal, Canada goose, curlew, redshank.

Leave the A4110 just south of Wigmore westwards on to an unclassified road through the forest. Take the track going eastwards nearly opposite the cemetery, but beware of deep ditches. Leave Wigmore northwards to Adforton and just before the village turn right. Keep right in half a mile to Criftin Ford Bridge and the River Teme.

Hertfordshire

BRAMFIELD FOREST   OS 147

The Forest is 4 miles north-west of Hertford and is one of the most productive areas of woodland in the county. It is owned by the Forestry Commission and is mixed deciduous and conifers. There is a wealth of woodland species in summer and redpolls are often present in huge flocks in winter when great grey shrikes are almost regular.

WINTER: redpoll, great grey shrike.

SUMMER: nightjar, long-eared owl, turtle dove, warblers, grasshopper warbler, redpoll.

Leave Hertford northwards on the A602 and turn left on the outskirts to Bramfield. 1 mile past the village, and in the forest, a wide path leads off to the north-east.

TRING RESERVOIRS   OS 159

The waters consist of Marsworth, Startops End, Tringford and Wilstone Reservoirs, lying 2 miles north of Tring and were created in the early years of the last century to serve the Grand Union Canal. They were built on the site of old marshes and relics of marsh flora are retained around their edges. They were made ornithologically famous by the breeding of little ringed plover in 1938, the first in Britain, and are now a National Nature Reserve. Wildfowl are quite numerous and waders are good on autumn passage. Black and commic terns are noted on both passages with sometimes large numbers of the former, and there is a small gull roost in winter.

WINTER: teal, wigeon, shoveler, pochard, tufted duck, goosander, gulls.

SPRING: waders, black terns.

SUMMER: great crested grebe.

AUTUMN: ringed and little ringed plovers, green and common sandpipers, greenshank, little stint, curlew sandpiper, black and commic terns.

Leave the A41 between Tring and Aylesbury northwards on the B489 at Aston Clinton. There are footpaths covering most possible views of all the waters.

Huntingdonshire

GRAFHAM WATER   OS 134
Also known as Diddington Reservoir, this is England's largest man-made lake covering 2½ square miles. It was officially opened in 1966 but birds were present in the winter 1965-6. Though its bird population has not settled down it has held a wide variety of wildfowl, including Bewick's swan.

WINTER: wildfowl, Bewick's swan.

SPRING AND AUTUMN: waders, terns.

Leave the A1 westwards at Buckden 3 miles south-west of Huntingdon, and follow signs to the many car park vantage points.

WOODWALTON FEN   OS 134
The Fen lies east of the A1 between Peterborough and Huntingdon and has been maintained as a reserve by the Society for the Promotion of Nature Reserves since 1919. It was declared a National Nature Reserve covering 514 acres in 1954. Though the main interests are aquatic plants and their associated insects, there is an interesting variety of breeding marshy birds.

SUMMER: sedge and grasshopper warblers.

A public footpath crosses the area northwards from Church End, but visitors are recommended to obtain a permit from the Nature Conservancy, 60 Bracondale, Norwich, NOR58B, Norfolk. Leave the A1 eastwards on the B1090 or B660 5–8 miles north of Alconbury.

Kent

CLIFFE   OS 172; HT +0:10 Sheerness
Cliffe lies at the western end of the north Kent marshes where the huge area of mud to the east narrows as the Thames turns southward. Though originally an area of rough pasture the extraction of clay for the cement industry has resulted in a series of flooded pits near the sea wall. These are a favourite resort of diving duck and hold exceptionally large numbers in hard weather.

Waders occur on the meadows, together with various predators and black terns frequently fly upstream at Lower Hope Point in autumn.

WINTER: tufted duck, pochard, scaup, merganser, pintail,

North Kent Marshes, Cliffe-High Halstow: showing the three major access routes and the ease of round tours. The central track is not advised for cars

smew, grebes, divers, waders, snow bunting, short-eared owl.
SPRING AND AUTUMN: waders, black tern, garganey.

Leave the A2 1 mile after its junction with the M2 at Strood, left on to the A289. After 1 mile turn left on to the B2000 to Cliffe. Pass straight through the village and turn left at the bottom. Bear right along a rough concrete road out to pits. Park near Coastguard Cottages and continue on foot beside pits to the sea wall. Walk northwards.

DUNGENESS   OS 184; HT −0:14 Dover
Dungeness has been a famous natural history site since the last century and is at present part RSPB reserve, part Dungeness Bird Observatory, and also the site of a Nuclear Power Station.

Dungeness is a shingle promontory jutting out into the Channel between Hastings and Folkestone, the shingle is some 18 feet thick and only barely above high tide mark. The area is a mass of ridges each of which represents a past beach with slacks between them in which most of the vegetation grows. These masses of gorse and brambles are attractive to the migrants which are concentrated by the geographical situation of the 'Ness. The RSPB reserve, covering 1,233 acres has the only two areas of natural water, the Open Pits, in the entire peninsula.

The main attraction is the migrants and the Observatory is thronged through spring and autumn by students of bird migration. The bushes harbour a variety of birds over 6,000 of which are caught annually. They include large numbers of the commoner chats, flycatchers and warblers as well as the rarer autumn visitors such as bluethroat and melodious warbler, and the true vagrants like Radde's, Pallas' and rufous warblers. Sea watching for migrants is usually good.

Dungeness is not dead in summer. It is the only breeding resort of the common gull in England, stone curlew breed on the shingle, and black redstarts on the power station.

WINTER: wigeon, teal, scoter, divers, grebes.

SPRING: wheatear, warblers, scoter, skuas, auks, gannet, waders.

SUMMER: common and herring gulls, common tern, wheatear, stone curlew, black redstart.

AUTUMN: chats, flycatchers, warblers, bluethroat, melodious warbler, skuas, scoter, gannet, Mediterranean gull, little gull, black tern, common, Arctic and roseate terns, rarities.

Leave Rye eastwards on the A259 and turn right in 1 mile to Camber Sands. Continue to Lydd and take the ring road to Dungeness. At Dungeness avoid forking left to the pub and keep right towards Old Light. The end cottage is the Observatory.

For the RSPB reserve parties meet the Warden at Boulderwall Farmhouse, but check this when applying for permit to the RSPB. At present they are only organized between 1st April and 1st September on Saturdays, Sundays, Wednesdays and Thursdays – cost 5s 0d.

Spartan accommodation at the Observatory is 6s 0d per night and must be booked in advance through H. A. R. Cawkell, 6 Canute Road, Hastings, Sussex.

HIGH HALSTOW AND EGYPT BAY
                                        OS 172; HT +0:05 Sheerness
This is the central area of the North Kent marshes and probably the best for those searching for large numbers of birds. The water meadows attract up to 1,500 white-fronts in the new year, and the fleets are used by wildfowl and passage waders. The foreshore, here over 1 mile wide, is the most attractive habitat. On a rising tide huge numbers of duck and waders are moved within range of the sea wall and concentrations occur particularly in Egypt and St Mary's Bays. The area also boasts the woodland of Northward Hill, which, though being primarily known for the large heronry (usually over a hundred nests) also holds the commoner woodland species.

WINTER: white-fronted goose, wigeon, pintail, shoveler, shelduck, knot, curlew, redshank.

SPRING: whimbrel, garganey.

SUMMER: shelduck, heron, long-eared owl.

AUTUMN: green and wood sandpipers, greenshank, little stint.

Leave the A2, 1 mile after its junction with the M2 at Strood, left on to the A289. In 2 miles join the A228 and after 4 miles turn left toward High Halstow. Take the first on the right, Decoy Hill Road, and halt where gate bars the way to motor vehicles. Turn right past the gate to St. Mary's Bay. Turn left on sea wall to Egypt Bay.

About half-way along Decoy Hill Road is the entrance to Northward Hill which is an RSPB reserve of 131 acres. Access is by free permit which is obtainable in advance from the RSPB.

See Map, page 60.

SANDWICH AND PEGWELL BAYS
                                        OS 173; HT +0:20 Dover
The two bays form the entrance to the Stour estuary on the east Kent coast between Ramsgate and Deal and are ideally

situated to receive continental migrants. This led to the establishment in 1961 of the Sandwich Bay Bird Observatory. Though passerines are of importance the area is well provided with inter-tidal sand which becomes rather muddier near the mouth of the Stour in Pegwell Bay. Behind the sand dunes lie the noted Sandwich Golf Links and between them and the river are areas of fresh marshes, the northern parts of which are attractive to migrant waders.

Wildfowl are not of great importance though both wild swans occur every year as do parties of white-fronted and brent geese. Divers and grebes frequent Pegwell Bay. Open shore waders are very plentiful in winter and passage is usually excellent.

WINTER: curlew, bar-tailed godwit, knot, redhank, golden plover, teal, swans, divers and grebes, hen harrier, snow bunting.

SPRING: waders, passerines, terns, rarities.

AUTUMN: whimbrel, green and wood sandpipers, greenshank, little stint, ruff, passerines, rarities.

Take the A256 or A257 to Sandwich. A toll is payable if coming southwards from Ramsgate. Leave eastwards on unclassified roads towards Sandwich Bay. Then:

1. Turn left on foot after 1 mile towards the Golf Club buildings and take the track off to the left just before the entrance. Continue and bear right towards the shore across the links or along the river bank out towards Pegwell Bay.

2. Continue straight on, paying the toll, to Sandwich Bay Estate and the Observatory at No. 1 Bungalow, Old Downs Farm. As an alternative to the above it is possible to walk northwards to Pegwell Bay along the beach.

Sandwich Bay Bird Observatory offers hostel type accommodation at 5s. 0d. per night. Write to J. N. Hollyer, 1 Woodland Way, Woodnesborough, Sandwich, Kent. Toll passes can be obtained at the same time as booking accommodation.

SHEPPEY AND THE SWALE

OS 172; HT −0:05 Sheerness at Harty Ferry

The Isle of Sheppey and the Swale channel forms a vast area of prime bird-watching on the north coast of the county. Intending visitors should note carefully which side of Kingsferry Bridge they wish to work (both are exceedingly attractive) as from Shell Ness to Seasalter is 3 miles direct and about 30 by road. The Swale is bordered by large mudflats on both banks especially near the mouth and above Fowley Island. The area forms one of the best for waders in the county and is the winter resort of up to 15,000 knot. Bar-tailed godwit, 500, and grey plover, 1,000, are more plentiful in late autumn, but are also present in winter.

Behind the protective sea walls are expanses of rough grazing intersected by dykes and fleets. These form the main haunts of wildfowl in the area, especially on the Sheppey shore. Sea duck are mainly found at the eastern end of the Swale off Shell Ness, and both white-fronted and brent geese are regular.

Freshwater waders are numerous in autumn and though they can be found on many fleets and marshes, Windmill Creek is the best.

Other birds in the area include as good a collection of predators in autumn and winter as one would find anywhere in southern England and a passage of skuas off Shell Ness in autumn.

WINTER: knot, bar-tailed godwit, oystercatcher, grey plover, turnstone, white-fronted and brent geese, wigeon, pintail, shoveler, merganser, eider, goldeneye, scoter, hen harrier, merlin, short-eared owl.

SPRING: green sandpiper, spotted redshank, garganey.

AUTUMN: black-tailed and bar-tailed godwits, grey plover, wood, green and curlew sandpipers, spotted redshank, greenshank, little stint, marsh harrier, skuas.

The route from London follows the A2 and the M2 at least as far as its junction with the A249. Thereafter a decision must be made between the various sites and access points. Access is as follows.

1. SHELL NESS: Leave the M2 at A249 signposted Sheppey and continue over Kingsferry Bridge (always worth a stop and a look at the Swale) to a roundabout at A250. Follow signposts to Leysdown and continue straight through until a gate with 'Private' notice bars the way. Walk directly to the sea across rough ground. Along this beach is a huge gathering of waders at high tide, with wildfowl offshore.

Turn southwards and walk along the beach to Shell Ness for more waders and especially sea duck. The area is a reserve of the Kent NT.

2. HARTY FERRY: A road southwards between Leysdown and Eastchurch is signposted 'Ferry Inn'. Turn down and continue for 1 mile before turning sharp left over Capel Fleet. This is always worth investigating for duck and autumn waders. The road then runs parallel to the fleet for another mile before turning right and then right again down to the Ferry Inn, for waders, duck and white-fronts.

3. WINDMILL CREEK AND DUTCHMAN'S ISLAND: The first track east of Eastchurch runs down to the marshes but the farmer's permission is needed. This area is now of very difficult access.

4. MURSTON: Leave Sittingbourne on the A2 eastwards to Bapchild, turn left and follow unclassified roads to Little Murston or to Blackletts and continue to the sea wall. Fowley Island is a favourite resort of mergansers.

5. CONYER: Leave the A2 at Teynham northwards on unclassified roads to Conyer. Continue past the inn and walk round works along the sea wall on the western side next to the creek. Turn eastwards past Fowley Island.

6. SOUTH HARTY FERRY: Leave the A2 to Faversham town centre. Leave westwards on an unclassified road to Oare and continue to Ferry. Turn westwards from here to Fowley Island, having obtained farmer's permission.

7. THE SOUTH OAZE: Take the M2 to its present southern end and junction with the A2, continue on to the A299 but turn first left on to B2040 and first right to Goodnestone, then continue to the sea. A path behind the inn runs westward on to the sea wall and gives excellent views of the huge foreshore. High tide is essential for waders and sea duck.

8. SEASALTER: Continue eastwards along the coast road after No 6 or leave the A299 (a continuation of the M2) left at Fox's Cross to Seasalter. Westwards lies the coast road to Graveney, and across the railway in the town centre and eastwards a footpath. Both provide waders at high tide.

STODMARSH   OS 173

Stodmarsh lies in the Great Stour valley some 4 miles downstream from Canterbury. Though doubtless always a marshy area it owes its real value to subsidence caused by the nearby coalmining activities at Chislet. An area of open water covering 500 acres, and an even larger area of reed beds has been created providing the largest fresh-marsh in Kent. The marsh is bisected by a wall running from the village to the river bank from which all the birds can be seen. In winter the valley further down is liable to flood near Grove Ferry and this area with the water at Stodmarsh is a great attraction to wildfowl. At the very end of the season in March there is an influx of garganey, often over 100.

WINTER: wigeon, teal, shoveler, pochard, pintail, gadwall, wild swans, hen harrier.

SPRING: ruff, garganey, marsh harrier.

SUMMER: sedge, reed and grasshopper warblers.

AUTUMN: migrants, hirundines, wagtails.

Leave Canterbury eastwards on the A257 and turn left after 1½ miles, on to unclassified roads to Stodmarsh. In the village turn left past the Red Lion at a tiny triangle of green down a farm track. Keep right, and after 300 yards turn right along a bank, across a dyke, and then left along the wall from which views can be obtained over the whole area. Do not leave the wall on to private land.

Stodmarsh: many watchers walk all the way to Grove Ferry relying on public transport for the return journey. Do not park at the entrance of the lane leading to the marsh

Lake District (Cumberland and Westmorland)

LAKELAND FELLS (Cumberland/Westmorland)
OS Tourist Lake District

The Fells lie at the heart of the Lake District centred on the Scafell area. Though noted for their beauty and as the centre of a National Park the Fells are not outstanding for birds, but do hold the bulk of breeding ravens and peregrines in northern England. Large numbers of the former gather at the top of Helvellyn. The usual upland species breed. The eastern fells are lonely and desolate and hold some of the most interesting species.

SUMMER: buzzard, peregrine, wheatear, ring ouzel, pied flycatcher, redstart, warblers.

The bird-watcher need not venture to the tops for his birds but some climbing up screes may be necessary for ring ouzels. Otherwise the valleys are best and none better than Borrowdale. South of Keswick on the B5289 walk from the Bowder Stone southwards, up Stonethwaite Beck for delicious woodland. Continue to Seatoller and walk up to Seathwaite past excellent woodland and then up to Sty Head with wheatears all the way. Grasmere is another good centre and Easedale has most of the typical species including ring ouzel above Easedale Tarn.

Youth Hostels are ideally situated and other accommodation ranges up to the highest quality. No one should venture on to the hills unprepared and without *Wainwright's Guide* to the appropriate area. These Guides are available in local shops and are invaluable to walkers.

RAVENGLASS (Cumberland)

OS 88; HT +0:05 Liverpool

A local nature reserve of 583 acres, situated on the Drigg Dunes which bar the mouth of the River Esk on its northern shore. The reserve was established in 1954 to protect the breeding colony of black-headed gulls, (6–8,000 pairs) the largest in Britain. A variety of other species breed, including four species of tern.

Wildfowl in winter are not outstanding but divers are quite frequent and the commoner waders are numerous.

WINTER: wigeon, goldeneye, divers, knot, peregrine.

SPRING: waders.

SUMMER: black-headed gull, common, Arctic, Sandwich and little terns, ringed plover, merganser, shelduck.

AUTUMN: knot, turnstone, whimbrel, greenshank, bar-tailed godwit.

The best method for a casual visit is by boat from Ravenglass just off the coastal A595 with permission from Cumberland County Council, The Courts, Carlisle, Cumberland. The village provides excellent views over the major part of the estuary area.

ST. BEES HEAD (Cumberland)   OS 82

St. Bees Head lies 2 miles south of Whitehaven. The high red sandstone cliffs are one of England's notable sea-bird breeding stations.

SUMMER: guillemot, razorbill, black guillemot, puffin, kittiwake, fulmar, raven.

Leave Whitehaven southwards on the B5345 and turn right

after 1½ miles to Sandwith. Follow unclassified roads as far as possible out to an OS height point 415, east of Tarnflat Hall. A footpath from here leads to the coast half a mile north of North Head, and the cliff edge footpath runs all the way round to South Head.

Lancashire

FAIRHAVEN-LYTHAM   OS 94; HT −0:04 Liverpool

Situated on the south-west corner of the Fylde at the mouth of the Ribble. The huge foreshore here is predominantly muddy and attracts a larger variety of waders than the St Anne's area. There are thousands of knot, black-tailed godwit number a thousand in autumn, and purple sandpipers are regular on the mussel beds. Thirteen species can usually be seen on a winter day. Snow buntings are regularly on the shore north of Fairhaven lake.

WINTER: knot, bar-tailed godwit, purple sandpiper, dunlin, shelduck, snow bunting.

SPRING: waders.

AUTUMN: black-tailed and bar-tailed godwits, turnstone, knot, purple sandpiper, whimbrel, passerine migrants.

Straightforward access from promenade, but for a quick look, park at Fairhaven Lake.

FOULNEY ISLAND   OS 88; HT −0:05 Liverpool

Situated near Walney Island in the south-west of the Lake District and is a mile long sandy-shingle promontory stretching southwards parallel to Walney. It was declared a nature reserve by the Lake District NT in 1963. Breeding birds include over 1,500 pairs of the four commoner terns. The Rampside Sands on the eastern side are a haunt of waders, grebes, divers and wildfowl.

WINTER: merganser, scoter, velvet scoter, scaup, pink-footed goose, waders, red-necked grebe, divers.

SPRING: waders, scoter.

SUMMER: common, Arctic, Sandwich and little terns.

AUTUMN: waders, terns, skuas.

Leave Barrow southwards on the A5087 and on reaching the coast turn right to Rampside. Continue past the village out towards Roa Island. For access to the reserve, apply to the Secretary, Lake District Naturalists' Trust, Rockgate, Levens, Kendal, Westmorland.

LEIGHTON MOSS OS 89

Leighton Moss lies 4 miles north of Carnforth near the village of Silverdale. Though used for pasture for over 200 years, wartime neglect of the pumping station allowed the land to revert to marshland and it has now been leased by the RSPB. A central causeway, which is a public footpath, divides Leighton from Storrs Moss, though both are part of the reserve. Storrs has a larger area of open water in spite of its greater distance from the sea. Areas of willow scrub with some oak and birch give way to sedges along the moss edge, while reeds are the typical habitat over the greater part of the area. The Society has recently created shallow edges to attract waders. Amongst an outstanding collection of breeding birds, the bittern is the centre of attraction, though the reed warbler here reaches its farthest north.

Winter brings wildfowl with quite large numbers of water rails.

WINTER: shoveler, pintail, water rail, redpoll.

SPRING: black tern, marsh harrier, waders.

SUMMER: bittern, shoveler, pochard, grasshopper and reed warblers, lesser whitethroat.

AUTUMN: waders, black tern, marsh harrier, great grey shrike, redpoll.

Permits are available together with arrangements for the current season from the RSPB at a cost of 5s. 0d. unescorted and 7s. 6d. escorted. The causeway begins near Silverdale Station on the road between Myers Farm and Yealand Storrs and lead eastwards. There is a public hide here giving good views over the reserve.

MORECAMBE BAY OS 89; HT +0:01 Liverpool

Morecambe Bay is the huge expanse of inter-tidal sand lying between Morecambe and Walney Island and is roughly 10 miles square. Counts of the birds of the area are few and necessarily rather rough, but *c.* 120,000 oystercatchers seems worth noting.

Here we are dealing with the stretch of coast from Heysham to Morecambe and Hest Bank where the immediate offshore shoals are rather narrow. Notable in a rather poor collection of wildfowl (the sands are a good roost but provide little wildfowl food) are sawbills and sea duck between Morecambe and Hest Bank. There are good numbers of waders.

WINTER: merganser, goosander, long-tailed duck, smew, goldeneye, pintail, shoveler, bar-tailed godwit, knot, oystercatcher, divers.

SPRING AND AUTUMN: whimbrel, greenshank, turnstone.

Almost the entire length of this shore is flanked by the A5105. At the Heysham end follow minor roads out to Lower Heysham, where a footpath runs along the shore. At Hest Bank cross the railway north of the station and walk northwards on a track along the edge of the saltings.

ST. ANNE'S – SQUIRE'S GATE
                              OS 94; HT −0:04 Liverpool
This stretch of beach runs north of St. Anne's pier on the south-west corner of the Fylde. The foreshore is sandy and stretches 3 miles into the Irish Sea, whereas south of Fairhaven the shore becomes increasingly muddy and attracts rather different species. Dominant in this stretch are winter concentrations of thousands of waders. Autumn brings large numbers of these species and terns into the area. With late autumn westerly gales, numbers of sea birds are blown on shore regularly, including shearwaters, skuas and both petrels. At Squire's Gate the shore is only half a mile wide and sea duck, divers and grebes can be seen quite regularly in autumn and winter.

WINTER: sanderling, redshank, knot, bar-tailed godwit, oystercatcher, eider, scoter, divers, grebes.

SPRING: waders.

AUTUMN: common, Arctic, Sandwich and little terns, sanderling, knot, godwit, oystercatcher, Arctic skua, petrels, shearwaters.

The whole area can be seen from the foreshore which is of open access in many places.

SOUTHPORT   OS 94 and 100; HT−0:26 Liverpool
Southport is on the southern shore at the mouth of the Ribble but the area included here covers the town and Marine Lake, the sandbanks at the mouth of the estuary that have been a National Wildfowl Refuge covering 14,300 acres, since 1956, the 3,000 acres of now drained Martin Mere, and the huge expanse of low lying mosses between Lydiate–Hightown and Southport–Scarisbrick. Pink-feet are the main attraction with 5,000 in autumn and 3,000 in winter roosting on the sands and feeding at Martin Mere and the mosses. Other wildfowl in this vast area includes a regular number of sea duck on Southport Marine Lake, and Hesketh Park Lake in Southport holds a variety of duck that come to roost. The muddy area around the pier attracts good numbers of waders.

WINTER: pink-footed goose, wigeon, pintail, shoveler, merganser, goldeneye, whooper swan, bar-tailed godwit, knot.

SPRING AND AUTUMN: waders.

The Marine Lake, the Pier and Hesketh Park are within a short walk of the mainline station. Martin Mere and the mosses and geese marshes can be reached by a number of roads, though the best idea is to wait for them to flight by the shore at Marine Lake.

WALNEY ISLAND   OS 88; HT −0:05 Liverpool

Situated at the south-west corner of the Lake District separated by only the narrow Walney Channel from industrial Barrow-in-Furness, to which it is linked by a bridge. The island is 8 miles long and the southern half has been declared a nature reserve by the Lancashire and Lake District NT. Breeding birds include the largest ground-nesting colony of lesser-black-backed and herring gulls in Europe, the southernmost breeding station of eiders in Britain, and a variety of other species. The area at the southern point together with Piel Island and Foulney is one of the largest wader roosts in Lancashire and thousands of birds can be counted at high tide. The island is also used as a bird observatory with a Heligoland trap and fair numbers of passage migrants are ringed. Skuas and terns are regularly noted offshore in autumn, and eiders are present offshore in large numbers almost throughout the year.

WINTER: oystercatcher, knot, eider, teal, wigeon, shelduck, divers, grebes.

SUMMER: herring and lesser black-backed gulls, eider, oystercatcher, ringed plover.

AUTUMN: waders, terns, skuas, passerine migrants.

Straightforward from Barrow. Access to the reserve is by permit, 2s. 6d. per visit, or 10s. 0d. per season. Cottage accommodation on hostel lines is available to genuine naturalists for 10s. 0d. per night or 40 s. 0d. per week plus permit. All applications, inquiries, etc., to the Secretary, South Walney Reserve Committee, 74 Queen Street, Barrow.

Leicestershire and Rutland

EYE BROOK RESERVOIR (Leics)   OS 133

The reservoir is 3 miles north-east of Corby, and was created by damming the stream of the same name in 1940 and now covers some 400 acres. It is 2 miles by 1 mile and reaches a maximum depth of 40 feet. The natural banks and gently shelving sides provide excellent feeding for a great variety of aquatic species and for the brown trout which have made the reservoir a favourite haunt for fishermen. Other than for this sport the reservoir is strictly protected and ranked eighth best for wildfowl in England. An area of marsh-like habitat has been created at the northern end near the inlet and this attracts both duck and waders and is always worth close scrutiny. The Rutland (eastern) side has been extensively planted with spruce, pine and other trees, providing a sanctuary for smaller birds.

The main attractions are the winter wildfowl with wigeon reaching a peak of 1,500 in January-February. Pintail once reached 450. Divers and geese are irregular but are seen most winters, and up to 50 Bewick's swans are now regular.

Eye Brook is also the best place in Leicester and Rutland for wader passage. Terns are regular and black terns pass through in spring and autumn.

WINTER: wigeon, pochard, goldeneye, pintail, shoveler, goosander, great crested grebe, gulls.

SPRING: waders, black terns.

AUTUMN: wood and green sandpipers, ruff, greenshank, little stint, duck, little grebe, terns.

The reservoir can be viewed without leaving the public highway but members of the Leicestershire and Rutland Ornithological Society can enter the plantation and marsh if carrying their membership card. Leave the A47 southwards at Uppingham on the A6003 to Caldicote or take that road northwards from Kettering. Turn westwards 50 yards north of the level-crossing at Caldecote to Stoke Dry and the reservoir.

STANFORD RESERVOIR (Leics/Northants)   OS 132

Situated some 6 miles north-east of Rugby and is 1 mile long with natural banks. Though not outstanding from the numbers point of view the water holds a wide selection of wildfowl, including a good flock of goosander. Summer birds include hirundines and wagtails and there is an autumn passage of waders and black terns.

WINTER: wigeon, shoveler, pochard, goosander, great crested grebe, cormorant.

AUTUMN: wood and green sandpipers, greenshank, black tern.

Leave Rugby eastwards on the A427 to Swinford. $1\frac{1}{2}$ miles past here turn sharp right and then left down to the reservoir dam. Access is by permit, obtainable from Rugby Joint Water Board, 50 Albert Street, Rugby. Views can be obtained from the road at the eastern end. Take the Welford Road out of Kilworth and view from ridge in half a mile.

Lincolnshire

GIBRALTAR POINT   OS 114; HT −0:22 King's Lynn
Situated on the northern shore at the mouth of the Wash, 3
miles south of Skegness. It is a local nature reserve and the site
of the Bird Observatory and Field Research Station. Though
the emphasis is on migration winter brings numbers of divers
and sea duck, while there is always a very large flock of snow
buntings, and a few shore larks and Lapland buntings. On passage waders in great variety pass through and terns and skuas
are noted offshore in some numbers. Passerines include chats,
warblers and flycatchers, often in dramatic numbers. Almost
anything can and does turn up.

WINTER: divers, sea duck, hen harrier, rough-legged buzzard,
great grey shrike, oystercatcher, bar-tailed godwit, knot,
shore lark, snow bunting, Lapland bunting.

SPRING: waders, chats, warblers.

SUMMER: little tern, ringed plover.

AUTUMN: pink-footed goose, whimbrel, bar-tailed godwit,
green and wood sandpipers, spotted redshank, curlew sandpiper, ruff, commic and black terns, skuas, chats, warblers,
flycatchers, rarities, diurnal migrants.

Leave Skegness southwards to Gibraltar Point. Accommodation is available on hostel lines at the Observatory, 7s. 6d. per
night. Bookings to the Secretary, Pyewipes, Willoughby,
Alford, Lincs.

See Map, page 74.

HOLBEACH   OS 124; HT −0:05 King's Lynn
This site lies on the south-western corner of the Wash, 8 miles
north of Holbeach on the A151. As in other parts of the Wash
new land is constantly being taken from the sea and provides
bird-watching of varying quality before it finally disappears
under the plough. The main interest at Holbeach lies on the
sea wall between Fotheringham House and Holbeach St.
Matthew and especially at the high tide roost of waders on
Flushing Creek Wall. During spring tides waders are forced
on to the fields behind the sea wall and have been caught by the
Wash Wader Ringing Group with rocket propelled nets. The
Flushing Creek wall is designed to funnel the tide and create a
scouring action along the sea wall and has prevented the build-
up of large areas of saltings at this point.

Vast assemblages of the commoner waders are the main
attraction but 'fresh' waders are regular in some numbers in

The Wash: showing the main access points. Only the four on the east coast and Gibraltar Point are worth visiting at all times. The other points are high tide specialities only

autumn on the numerous dykes. The only other species of interest are wildfowl with large numbers of duck and a November roost of pink-feet.

AUTUMN: knot, dunlin, grey plover, turnstone, bar-tailed godwit, green, wood and curlew sandpipers, little stint, greenshank, ruff, short-eared owl.

WINTER: knot, dunlin, grey plover, turnstone, short-eared owl, hen harrier, wigeon, pink-footed goose.

Leave the A17 at Chapelgate northwards on to the B1359. Leave this to the left after 2½ miles signposted Holbeach St Matthew. Continue through the village and along banks to a Police Notice liberally sprinkled with gun shot wounds. On foot northwards to the sea wall and then out past a wildfowler's barge to Flushing Creek Wall.

London

Far all places mentioned in this chapter readers should refer to Map, page 76.

BARN ELMS RESERVOIRS   OS 170

Barn Elms is rated tenth best for wildfowl in England and lies very close to central London alongside the Thames on the southern side of Hammersmith Bridge.

Duck are always present in large numbers in even the mildest winters and diving duck regularly reach four figures. At one time Barn Elms was 'the' London locality for smew but numbers in recent years have been very small and watchers looking for this species would be well advised to go elsewhere.

Other species of interest are terns, including black, on both spring and autumn passage, and usually an interesting trickle of the commoner waders. A small disused gravel pit behind the pumping station at the entrance end is often interesting.

WINTER: tufted duck, pochard, gadwall, wigeon, smew.

SPRING AND AUTUMN: black and common tern, waders.

On the southern side of Hammersmith Bridge turn eastwards at traffic lights along Merthyr Terrace. Access is strictly by permit only from Metropolitan Water Board, New River Head, Roseberry Avenue, EC1. Permits entitle holder to visit several London reservoirs. They are available only to *bona fide* watchers aged over 21. Some evidence of seriousness is required, viz. membership of London Natural History Society, BTO or RSPB.

RAINHAM MARSH (Essex)   OS 161

The marsh lies on the northern bank of the Thames at Erith Reach below Dagenham. Though basically an area of water meadows they have been changed recently by the pumping of mud slurry dredged from the Thames into an embanked section, and the creation of a rubbish tip. The main attraction is the brackish pools of mud and the condition of these is largely dependent, like sewage farms, on the activities of the authorities involved, in this case the Port of London Authority. At passage periods gatherings of waders are often large and exciting. Little ringed plover are regular in both spring and autumn.

WINTER: duck, short-eared owl.

SPRING: little ringed plover.

AUTUMN: little ringed plover, sandpipers, spotted redshank, little stint, shelduck.

London Area showing position of best areas in relation to the main arterial roads. Note the huge area of reservoirs in the Lea Valley between the A10 and A11 are almost entirely of restricted access

Take the A13 from central London through to Dagenham. Some 2 miles further turn right to Rainham Village and turn right in to Ferry Lane soon after the church. Continue for 1 mile to the factory area and then continue on foot along the riverbank to the marshes.

STAINES RESERVOIR   OS 160

The 424 acres of the Staines reservoirs are rated ninth amongst English top reservoirs from a wildfowl angle. It is one of the most intensively worked areas in the country and one may expect to meet more bird-watchers along the central causeway than almost anywhere else. Sunday is 'the' day and though the attractions are seasonal, there is always someone else about.

Throughout the winter duck are present in large numbers and the variety is the best in the London area, the reservoirs are also a good place during passage periods when waders are regularly present in small numbers. Influxes of black terns in spring tend to be large but in autumn this species is regularly present in August. Both waders and terns have included some first rate rarities in recent years. Amongst the most interesting birds to be seen at Staines at any time of the year is the regular flock of black-necked grebes during August-October.

WINTER: smew, goosander, wigeon, shoveler, goldeneye, tufted duck, pochard.

SPRING: black tern.

AUTUMN: black tern, commic tern, black-necked grebe, little gull, rarities.

Take the A30 to the Bulldog, turn right (northwards) along B378 parallel to the reservoir bank and stop after half a mile at a footpath leading up to the causeway that divides the reservoirs. Alternatively, continue southward for 2 miles after visiting Perry Oaks Sewage Farm.

STOKE NEWINGTON RESERVOIRS   OS 160

Less than 4 miles from St. Pauls between Seven Sisters Road, A503 and Stamford Hill, A10. There are two small pools with artificial banks surrounded by small areas of grass. In a normal winter the reservoirs hold a number of diving duck and always a quite sizeable flock of smew. In hard weather these relatively small pools stay ice-free longer than the other waters of the London area and at such times several thousand birds have been counted.

WINTER: tufted duck, pochard, smew, great crested grebe.

Leave Seven Sisters Road on the first turning southwards immediately east of Manor House. Woodbury Grove leads in to Lordship Road. There is no access but both pools can be seen from the aqueduct bridge and between the concrete railings on the north side.

WALTON HEATH (Surrey)   OS 170

The Heath lies on the gentle northward slope of the North Downs between the A217 and the B2032. Though a large part of it has been turned into a golf course, there remain large areas of birch and bracken, with conifer plantations, and thorn thickets. The area is a good breeding haunt of warblers, and a variety of heathland species. It is a regular haunt of great grey shrike in autumn and winter.

SUMMER: redpoll, willow tit, nightjar, warblers.

AUTUMN: great grey shrike.

Leave London on the A217 and fork right on to the B2032 at Banstead. Park off the road after 1¼ miles and walk up alongside the golf course.

Isle of Man

CALF OF MAN BIRD OBSERVATORY   OS 87

The Calf of Man is a small island at the southern tip of Man covering 616 acres, and belongs to the National Trust. Since 1952 the Calf has been administered by the Manx NT as a nature reserve and bird observatory. Among the breeding birds are large colonies of sea birds on the slate cliffs, and hooded crow and chough.

On passage passerines are noted in good numbers and regularly include the odd rarity.

SPRING: whimbrel, turnstone, warblers, chats, Manx shearwater, gannet.

SUMMER: kittiwake, razorbill, guillemot, fulmar, puffin, hooded crow, chough.

AUTUMN: whimbrel, turnstone, warblers, chats, Manx shearwater, gannet, rarities.

Day visitors are free to land on the Calf and should make arrangements with the boatmen at Port St. Mary or Port Erin. The trip can be arranged with the Calf's regular boatman and costs about 10s. 0d. An independent charter might cost £3 10s. 0d. Visitors to the observatory should obtain full details from the Secretary, The Manx Museum, Douglas. A resident warden is in charge of the old farmhouse which accommodates up to 10 visitors on hostel lines.

DERBYHAVEN, LANGNESS, CASTLETOWN BAY
OS 87

A narrow isthmus separates the two sandy bays and joins the rocky Langness area to the south-eastern corner of the island, near Castletown. Waders on passage can be numerous, especially in autumn. Derbyhaven is the best place on the island for divers, notably great northern, and there are always a few wildfowl about. Choughs regularly feed on the seaweed along the shoreline in winter.

Cley and Blakeney: the East Bank is the most famous bird-walk in Britain and is excellent for waders. Blakeney Point can be reached on foot along the shore path and by boat from Morston-Blakeney

WINTER: waders, great northern diver, chough.
SPRING: turnstone, terns.
AUTUMN: curlew, turnstone, knot, bar-tailed godwit, sanderling, curlew sandpiper, little stint, terns.

Leave Castletown on the A12 along Castletown Bay to Derbyhaven. Turn left for the Bay, and right for Langness. Paths and tracks lead north and south along the golf course.

Apply to the Castletown Commissioners for the *Tourist Guide*.

SPANISH HEAD AND CHASMS   OS 87

Spanish Head is the extreme south-eastern point of the Isle of Man and lies just across Calf Sound from the Calf of Man. The area of 256 acres of clifftop moorland is the property of the Manx NT. The cliffs rise to 300 feet and are the breeding site of many species.

SUMMER: auks, fulmar, raven, chough, hooded crow.

Leave Port St. Mary on the A31 to Cregneish which makes the ideal centre for a round walk of the clifftop footpath. A boat trip under the cliffs can be arranged from Port St. Mary, which has a wintering flock of purple sandpipers.

Apply to the Town Commissioners, Port St. Mary, for brochure.

Norfolk

BLAKENEY POINT AND HARBOUR AND
MORSTON SALTINGS

                          OS 125; HT +0:12 King's Lynn

This large area lying immediately north of the coastal A149 consists of three distinct habitats. The Point, the Harbour north of the main channel, the beach as far as Cley, and the saltings immediately north of Blakeney village, amounting to some 1,335 acres, are the property of the National Trust, which maintains the dunes and shingle system of the Point as a bird sanctuary. Roughly 1 mile square, the point is extensively used by the public yet still holds 1,000 pairs of common terns. It is also ideally situated to receive passerine migrants and large falls occur most autumns, these naturally include a number of rarities.

Blakeney Harbour itself is the haunt of numerous waders, especially during autumn and winter. Brent geese reach a peak of up to 2,000 in January–February, the occasional rare grebe turns up, and the osprey is almost a regular autumn visitor.

The stretch of saltings between Morston and Blakeney hold a regular flock of up to 70 Lapland buntings.

The Norfolk Broads: particular attention is drawn to the northern group which forms one of the most important wetland habitats in the country

Labels on map:
N

Horsey Mere
Martham Broad
Caister
Great Yarmouth
Breydon Water
4 miles
A1064
River Bure
Ormesby Broad
A149
River Thurne
Hickling Broad
Buckenham Broad
Rockland Broad
South Walsham Broad
Ranworth Broad
A47
Hoveton Lt. Broad
Woodbastwick Fen & Marshes
Barton Broad
Surlingham Broad
Wroxham Broad
Hoveton Gt. Broad
A1151

WINTER: brent goose, wigeon, bar-tailed godwit, turnstone, knot, dunlin, Lapland bunting, twite.

SUMMER: common and little terns, ringed plover, shelduck.

AUTUMN: godwits, turnstone, spotted redshank, passerines, migrants, rarities.

Blakeney point has no restrictions on access, though visitors are asked to avoid the terneries and be careful in summer. It is a 3½ mile walk over shingle to the point from Cley Coastguards. Boats run regularly from both Blakeney and Morston and there is a tea-room.

The harbour is best viewed from the north either from the point or from the Hood and the Marrams along the beach to Cley.

The saltings are best worked from the Morston end; taking a bus from Blakeney to Morston and walking back along the saltings is ideal. Turn north on the only turning in that direction in Morston from the A149. On reaching the first creek turn right and continue along a well worn (and wet) path across the saltings.

The whole area is reached by the coastal A149.

BREYDON WATER

OS 126; HT +0:01 Lowestoft at Yarmouth Bridge

Breydon forms the estuary of the Rivers Waveney, Yare and Bure, and lies immediately inland from Great Yarmouth on the county boundary with Suffolk. It is 3 miles by 1 mile, and is the haunt of numbers of waders, wildfowl, and other species. Brent, white-fronts and pink-feet are regular and bean geese and Bewick's swans are erratic visitors. Winter waders are numerous and passerines always include twite and snow bunting, and sometimes Lapland bunting.

A wide variety of waders and predators occur in autumn. Black terns are noted on both passages and spoonbills and avocets are seen most years.

WINTER: wigeon, shelduck, pintail, shoveler, scaup, golden-eye, brent, white-fronted and pink-footed geese, Bewick's swan, knot, grey plover, marsh and hen harriers, merlin, peregrine, short-eared owl, snow bunting, twite, Lapland bunting.

SPRING: whimbrel, spotted redshank, godwits, ruff, black tern, spoonbill, avocet.

AUTUMN: whimbrel, spotted redshank, godwits, ruff, green and wood sandpipers, curlew sandpiper, grey plover, marsh harrier, short-eared owl.

Cross Yarmouth bridge and immediately turn right through

houses and a maze of roads to the railway bridge. Pass under-
neath and walk along the southern shore for 3 miles to Burgh
Castle. Alternatively start the other end turning right past
Burgh Castle Church, for more countrified surroundings.

See Map, page 81.

THE BROADS   OS 126

The Broads are a series of freshwater lakes lying mainly in the
valleys of the Norfolk rivers that eventually drain into Breydon
Water and thus into the sea at Yarmouth. They are much reclaimed and overgrown with reeds, but still form a truly huge
expanse of wetland. Though originally thought of as a vast
silted up estuary, contemporary research has shown the
Broads to be a series of pools created by man's peat digging
activities. Most of them lie alongside rather than on the rivers,
and several of them show parallel banks that have been left
uncut, and which give rise to a series of islands in the open
water.

Thousands of people hire motor boats and spend their
holidays cruising the miles of connected waterways, yet the
disturbance to the marshes is generally slight. Indeed the area
remains very difficult to 'work' and in many cases access by
water is far freer than by land. Out of season boats are cheap
to hire, the birds are generally undisturbed and a splendid
bird-watching holiday can be enjoyed in either spring or
autumn. Esso publish a *Cruising Guide to the Norfolk Broads
and Rivers*, price 1s. 0d., which clearly shows which broads are
accessible by boat. They incidentally include Hickling and
Horsey.

1. *Bure Marshes National Nature Reserve:* The reserve lies
in the Bure Valley between Acle and Hoveton and covers over
1,000 acres of broad, reed marsh, fen and woodland. Declared
in 1958 and owned partly by the Norfolk NT the reserve includes Ranworth and Cockshoot Broads, Woodbastwick Fen,
and Hoveton Little Broad. Amongst an interesting collection
of birds is a flock of feral greylags numbering 400, and feral
flocks of Canada and Egyptian geese. Bearded tits are outstanding amongst an interesting collection of breeding species.

WINTER: feral greylag, Canada and Egyptian geese, gadwall,
wigeon, pochard, cormorant.

SUMMER: common tern, bearded tit, sedge and reed warblers, teal, shoveler.

Access is by permits which are strictly limited: apply to the
Nature Conservancy, 60 Bracondale, Norwich, NOR58B.

2. *Hickling Broad:* Hickling is one of the largest broads and

lies north of Potter Heigham, 3 miles from the sea. It was declared a National Nature Reserve in 1958 but has been a reserve,
largely owned by the Norfolk Naturalists' Trust, since 1945.
The present reserve covers 1,204 acres of open water, reed
marsh and fen and is an outstanding bird area at all seasons.
Spring and autumn bring a host of passage waders, and black
terns are regular. Breeding birds are quite outstanding though
both harriers have deserted the area.

WINTER: wigeon, shoveler, pochard, goldeneye, gadwall,
pintail, mute and Bewick's swans, marsh and hen harriers,
short-eared owl.
SPRING: black and common terns, grey plover, black-tailed
godwit, spotted redshank, green and wood sandpipers, ruff.
SUMMER: garganey, bittern, heron, bearded tit, common
tern, sedge, reed and grasshopper warblers.
AUTUMN: marsh harrier, short-eared owl, black-tailed godwit, sandpipers, greenshank, spotted redshank, ruff, black
tern, wildfowl.

Though a reserve, sailing and use of the broad are unrestricted. Access can be obtained at the north-western corner
southwards from Hickling village, and from the north side at
Hill Common. Permits are required to visit the Sanctuary area
and these are obtainable from The Norfolk NT, 4 The Close,
Norwich, NOR 16P at 10s. 0d., 5s. 0d. under 18.

3. *Horsey Mere:* Horsey is the property of the National
Trust and one of the most famous of the East Anglian bird
resorts. The Mere covers 120 acres and is surrounded by extensive reed beds. Its position, $1\frac{1}{2}$ miles from the sea, has added to
its attractions. Winter brings large numbers of wildfowl, including occasional herds of Bewick's swans, and hen and marsh
harriers are noted. Waders pass through but in neither the
number nor variety as on the Hickling wader grounds. Bearded
tit, water rail, bittern and short-eared owl breed. Marsh and
Montagu's harriers are regularly noted but do not now breed.
Autumn brings a return passage of waders with terns, and a
variety of passerines, hawks, etc.

WINTER: wigeon, pochard, goldeneye, Bewick's swan, hen
and marsh harriers, hooded crow, great grey shrike.
SPRING: ruff.
SUMMER: bearded tit, water rail, bittern, sedge, reed and
grasshopper warblers, short-eared owl, stonechat.
AUTUMN: waders, terns, passerines, harriers.

Leave the A149 1 mile north of Rollesby eastwards on the
B1152 to Martham. Continue via B1159 to Horsey. Access is by

application to Mr G. Crees, Swiss Cottage, Horsey; though some of the area can be seen from the windmill on the left half a mile before the village.

4. *Rockland Broad*: Rockland lies in the Yare Valley, 8 miles east of Norwich. Its 48 acres are the largest area of open water left in the valley, and though greatly disturbed it does have a definite attraction. Wildfowl are present throughout the winter but February, especially if severe, brings herds of both wild swans and often quite large numbers of smew, goosander and scaup. Spring passage occasionally brings numbers of black terns.

WINTER: wigeon, pochard, tufted duck, smew, goosander, scaup, whooper and Bewick's swans.

SPRING: black tern.

Leave Norwich south-eastwards on the A146 and after crossing the Yare fork left on to unclassified roads through Bramerton to Rockland St. Mary. The path round the south side of the Broad begins at the New Inn at the far end of the village.

CLEY AND SALTHOUSE MARSHES   OS 125

There can hardly be a serious bird-watcher in the country who has not made the pilgrimage to Cley. It has been the Mecca of ornithologists for the last 140 years during which over 275 distinct species have been recorded within the parish boundaries, including a most remarkable list of rarities. Cley and Salthouse lie at the eastern end of the long stretch of marshes and tidal saltings that guard the north Norfolk coast, and provide the most extensive area of fresh marsh on the whole coastline. Yet this alone does not account for the remarkable attraction that the area has for birds. It is perhaps its geographical position, at the point where the Norfolk coast begins to run directly east to west, that is the dominant factor. Whatever the causes, the East Bank at Cley is the best place in England to see passage waders – and to meet wellknown bird-watchers.

The main bird-watching areas lie between the villages of Cley and Salthouse and between the sea and the A149. The large shingle beach protects a series of semi-saline lagoons, the best of which are those known as Arnold's Marsh lying immediately east of the East Bank. This area of 29 acres is owned by the National Trust and is administered by the Norfolk NT which owns the 435 acres forming Cley Marshes proper on the other side of the East Bank. Gradually the open lagoons give way to a series of reed fringed pools with large reed beds and fields of rough grazing. The eastern end of Blakeney Harbour lies behind the beach to the west of Cley but I have included the area up to the western end of the Marrams.

Immediately behind the beach, west of the Cley Coastguard Station, are several areas of sueda bushes providing immediate cover to incoming migrants. The area of elder, brambles and osiers at Walsey Hills on the Salthouse boundary used to be used by Cley Bird Observatory as a trapping station and the disused Heligoland traps can still be seen.

Cley's specialities are unusual birds, migrants and vagrants of all shapes and sizes as well as an interesting collection of breeding marsh birds. Little gulls are daily in autumn, and the beach holds shore larks, and huge wintering flocks of snow buntings from October onwards. The lagoons are the haunt of waders throughout the year. Black-tailed godwits and ruffs usually manage to stay late and display in May.

The reeds and open pools provide Cley's main attractions during the breeding season with bearded tits quite numerous. On passage, marsh and Montagu's harriers quarter the reed beds and spoonbills are often seen in autumn.

WINTER: wigeon, shoveler, brent goose, snow bunting, shore lark, waders.

SPRING: ruff, black tern, fulmar, waders.

SUMMER: bearded tit, bittern, sedge and reed warblers, water rail, garganey.

AUTUMN: curlew, wood and green sandpipers, little stint, marsh and Montagu's harriers, snow bunting, shore lark, little gull, three skuas, eider, terns, rarities, bluethroat, barred warbler, Mediterranean gull, waxwing.

The A149 runs through Cley and Salthouse.

The Norfolk NT Sanctuary is equipped with several hides providing first class views over the whole reserve. Permits are available every day except Mondays, at 10s. 0d. (half-price under 18) from The Secretary, Norfolk NT, 4 The Close, Norwich, NOR16P. Unsold permits of a day's quota may be obtained from the Warden at Cley after 10 a.m. on the day concerned.

See Map, page 79.

HOLME AND THORNHAM HARBOUR
OS 124; HT −0:15 King's Lynn

Holme is strategically sited on the north Norfolk Coast just as it turns southwards into the Wash. It is ideally situated to receive migrants, a fact which is enhanced by a small plantation of pines and scrub on the immediate landward side of the coastal dunes. This is the only cover for a mile or more. Redbreasted flycatchers are almost annual visitors, and there was once a yellow-browed warbler and a Pallas's warbler in the same tree within 5 days of one another. The usual small passerine migrants are often plentiful. The Broad Water behind the dunes and pines has an extensive reed bed that regularly fills up with bearded tits in autumn, and this species has recently started to breed here. The muddy edges prove an attraction to numerous waders, as does the shore itself. At high tide waders pass eastwards in huge numbers to roost on Thornham Island which can be seen from the eastern end of the high dune system. These movements continue throughout the winter when knot are estimated to number over 25,000.

WINTER: knot, bar-tailed godwit, sanderling, brent goose, great grey shrike, hen harrier, short-eared owl, Lapland and snow buntings, shore lark.

SPRING: Bewick's swan, bar-tailed godwit, terns, passerines.

SUMMER: little tern, ringed plover, oystercatcher, grasshopper warbler, red-backed shrike, bearded tit.

AUTUMN: bar-tailed godwit, grey plover, whimbrel, knot, little stint, wood and green sandpipers, spotted redshank, passerines, chats, flycatchers, bearded tit, rarities.

Leave the A149 northwards at Thornham on to a track out to the old jetty. A sea wall on the western side leads out to Thornham Harbour and the dunes overlooking Broad Water and the sea. The Norfolk NT has recently purchased the area and inquiries should be addressed to The Warden, The Firs, Holme, King's Lynn. The Holme Observatory works part of the area: address, Holme Bird Observatory, Holme-next-the-Sea, King's Lynn.

See Map, page 74.

SCOLT HEAD ISLAND   OS 125; HT −0:15 King's Lynn

The island lies offshore between Brancaster and Burnham Overy, stretches 3½ miles from east to west, and covers 1,821 acres. It has been a National Nature Reserve since 1954. The birds of the area are varied and provide excitements at all seasons. Outstanding are the breeding colonies of terns, which include 1,400 pairs of Sandwich and 600 of common.

Winter brings good numbers of wildfowl with the flock of up to 850 brent geese that feed around Cockle Bight being the main attraction, along with huge numbers of waders.

Passage brings a large variety of waders, terns including roseate, kittiwakes especially in July and a fair number of passerines.

WINTER: brent goose, wigeon, goldeneye, merganser, eider,

knot, turnstone, bar-tailed godwit, grey plover, hen harrier, merlin, short-eared owl, twite.

SUMMER: common, Sandwich and little terns, short-eared owl, oystercatcher, shelduck.

AUTUMN: bar-tailed godwit, whimbrel, spotted redshank, turnstone, grey plover, short-eared owl, peregrine, roseate, and other terns, kittiwake.

Access is by boat, or by foot with care at low tide from Brancaster Staithe which is on the main A149; watch out for signpost 'To Scolt Head'. There are no restrictions on landing and one is free to roam everywhere except over the terneries during the breeding season. It is, however, wise to contact the Reserve Warden at Dial House, Brancaster Staithe, King's Lynn, Norfolk.

WELLS-NEXT-THE-SEA   OS 125; HT −0:16 King's Lynn

Wells was for long noted as 'the' haunt of geese on the Norfolk coast, up to 8,000 pink-feet having wintered in the area for at least a hundred years prior to 1938. This habit was destroyed by various war-time measures, including artillery practice and the ploughing up of the grassland leys which provided feeding grounds. Since then Wells has largely been noted for its waders and the flock of up to 1,000 brent that winter on the tidal flats.

The Lifeboat Station, which is the best place to observe the area, is backed by a plantation of pines that is strictly private and fenced by the Holkham Estate. Across the caravan site is a lake with an interesting reed bed. A path between the pines and lake is marked 'Exit Only' and the area is best approached from the Holkham Gap end.

At Holkham Gap the pine plantations stretch away along the dunes to east and west. The right hand group is freely accessible, easy to work, and is backed by birch, elder and bramble scrub that is attractive to small passerine migrants.

WINTER: brent goose, turnstone, bar-tailed godwit, oyster-catcher.

AUTUMN: migrants, goldcrest.

Wells is on the coastal A149. From the main road follow signpost 'Wells Quay and Town Centre', turn left at the quay and continue northwards with the high sea wall on right.

Northamptonshire

HOLLOWELL RESERVOIR   OS 133

The Reservoir lies alongside the A50 10 miles north of Northampton and covers 50–60 acres. Though less than 5 miles from Pitsford, this reservoir is important in its own right and is ranked fifth in England and Wales. The commoner duck have maxima of several hundred, while shoveler and goldeneye reach good figures.

WINTER: wigeon, pochard, shoveler, goldeneye, pintail, goosander, smew.

SUMMER: great crested and little grebes, sedge warbler, redshank.

Leave Northampton northwards on the A50 and after 9 miles turn left to Hollowell. Fork right in the village and continue towards Guisborough, looking right over the reservoir at a distance. Day permits are available with 24 hours notice from The Engineer and Manager, Mid-Northants Water Board, Cliftonville, Northampton.

PEAKIRK WATERFOWL GARDENS AND BOROUGH FEN DECOY

OS 123

Placed on the western boundary of the fenland about 6 miles north of Peterborough, just east of the main A15. The area is owned by the Wildfowl Trust and a series of shallow pools have been created which house an impressive collection of wildfowl. Only Peter Scott's *Wildfowl of the World* will enable you to identify all you see, which includes whooper swans, redbreasted geese, Barrow's goldeneye, etc. It is an excellent place to mug up your identification of rare vagrants from foreign parts, or merely to enjoy a good look at what elsewhere are often only specks on the reservoir.

Wild birds include a large colony of collared doves that subsist largely on the grain provided for the wildfowl; they breed from March to November. Wild duck, particularly shoveler, visit the grounds.

The decoy at Borough Fen, 2 miles away, is one of the oldest in the country and has been used for ringing duck since 1949. The pool covers $2\frac{1}{2}$ acres and is set in a secluded wood of 14 acres. It has 8 pipes, and often over a thousand ducks come in to roost. It is usually open to visitors during one weekend in May.

RESIDENT: wildfowl, duck, geese.

Leave the A15 5 miles north of Peterborough at Glinton eastwards to Peakirk. Watch out for a sign on the left in the village to 'Peakirk Waterfowl Gardens' along Chestnut Close. Admission is daily, times varying according to the season, at 3s. 6d. for adults with a reduction for children. Members of the

Wildfowl Trust enter free and may take a guest. The Gardens are open daily at 9.30 (12.00 a.m. Sunday, except for members) and close at 6.30 p.m. in summer and half an hour before sunset in winter.

PITSFORD RESERVOIR   OS 133

The Reservoir cover 800 acres, was flooded in 1955, and lies 8 miles north of Northampton. Apart from the dam and central causeway the banks are natural and gently shelving. Wildfowl are very numerous making this the fourth best reservoir in the country. Pochard have found conditions ideal and have numbered up to 2,000 and other common species are present in good numbers. Bewick's swans are regular and a few geese are recorded annually.

Wader passage is good and autumn also brings terns, including black terns.

WINTER: pochard, wigeon, shoveler, pintail, goldeneye, Bewick's swan, geese.

SPRING: waders.

AUTUMN: little ringed plover, grey plover, green and wood sandpipers, knot, curlew sandpiper, ruff, black and commic terns.

Leave Northampton northwards on the A50 and keep right after 2 miles on the A508. Turn right at Brixworth and obtain distant views over the reservoir from the road. Later at the causeway look north and south over about half the total water. Permits are required for access. The Recorder for Birds of the Northants Natural History and Field Club holds four transferable permits; apply to him at 1 Tenby Road, Northampton.

Northumberland and Durham

BAMBURGH-SEAHOUSES (N'land)
                                     OS 71; HT −0:51 River Tyne

This is a stretch of sandy coastline 3 miles long, interrupted here and there by rocky stretches, notably at Stag Rocks, Monk's House and Seahouses. The Farne Islands lie less than 2 miles offshore and dominate the sea view. The entire stretch is very good in winter and Slavonian and red-necked grebes, all three divers, and sea duck are all comparatively common, especially off Stag Rocks.

A variety of waders occurs on autumn passage when sea birds are seen offshore. Arctic skuas are seen almost daily in summer and in autumn are sometimes very numerous, and great skuas are quite frequent. Terns include all five British breeding species.

Passerine migration is very good in autumn and was extensively studied at Monk's House Observatory. The commoner warblers, chats and flycatchers annually include a mixture of less usual species.

WINTER: divers, Slavonian and red-necked grebes, long-tailed duck, scoter, velvet scoter, eider, purple sandpiper, sanderling, turnstone, knot.

SUMMER: terns, Arctic skua.

AUTUMN: sanderling, turnstone, little stint, Arctic and great skuas, gannet, terns, roseate tern, warblers, chats, flycatchers.

The whole area of foreshore from the coastal B1340 is of free public access the southern half belonging to the National Trust. The entire area can and does produce birds but Stag Rocks, called Islestone on OS is best for sea birds, especially in winter. Monk's House should be visited.

Bamburgh lies at the eastern end of the B1342 and B1341 which leave the A1 south of Belford.

CRESSWELL PONDS (N'land)   OS 71 and 78

The ponds are on the coast 4 miles north of Ashington and 1 mile north of Cresswell. They are of recent origin due to min-

Cresswell Ponds: an area particularly attractive to all types of migrant ing subsidence and their proximity to the sea makes them attractive to a large variety of waders and other migrants. Over 180 species have been noted in 10 years including a fair number of rarities. The area around the ponds is mainly water meadows. There is also a considerable growth of hedge that is attractive to passerine migrants.

The foreshore is frequented by many waders, and terns are often numerous offshore in summer, as are sea duck in winter. Passerines including the commoner chats, flycatchers and warblers are found in the small mixed woodland south-west of the main pond.

WINTER: turnstone, sanderling, purple sandpiper, scaup, scoter, long-tailed duck, eider, merganser, snow bunting.

SPRING: green sandpiper.

SUMMER: commic and roseate terns.

AUTUMN: ruff, spotted redshank, whimbrel, wood sandpiper, curlew sandpiper, little stint, terns, black tern, skuas, great skua, chats, flycatchers, warblers.

Leave Ashington westwards on the A197 and on the outskirts turn north on to the A1068 to Ellington. Turn right and left to Cresswell village and turn left again along the coast road from which good views can be obtained of the shore, the sea and the ponds. Three footpaths lead inland, but see map.

The area is heavily shot over, largely by unauthorised gunners. All the ponds are on private land.

FARNE ISLANDS (N'land)   OS 71

The Farnes consist of some 30 islands lying 2–5 miles offshore near Bamburgh. The majority of the islands belong to the National Trust and are of straightforward public access. They have long been a bird-watchers' Mecca and annually attract large numbers of observers to see the breeding seabirds. Four species of tern breed annually, including the rare roseate.

Passage periods bring a variety of waders, and sea watching is good with divers, shearwaters and skuas, though as an observatory the islands have so far not enjoyed the full daily coverage that is needed in autumn. Nevertheless, chats, warblers and flycatchers are often quite numerous and rarities are occasionally seen.

Amongst the oddities are the small party of greylag geese that spend late summer on the outer isles.

SPRING: turnstone, whimbrel, divers, skuas, scoter.

SUMMER: common, Arctic, Sandwich and roseate terns, cormorant, shag, eider, guillemot, razorbill, puffin, oystercatcher, ringed plover, fulmar, kittiwake.

AUTUMN: terns, eider, scoter, whimbrel, turnstone, knot, purple sandpiper, divers, Manx shearwater, Arctic and great skuas, chats, warblers, flycatchers, rarities.

The islands are reached by motor boat from Seahouses and a landing fee of 3s. 6d. is charged for non-members of the National Trust. Intending visitors should obtain permits from the Post Office, Bolton's Garage or from the Farne Islands Committee, Narrowgate House, Alnwick. The Brownsman is closed to visitors during the breeding season, though all the species there can be seen on The Inner Farne which is the best island.

A great deal of ringing is undertaken by the Northumberland and Durham Natural History Society and a report on the Islands is included in that Society's annual report.

GRINDON LOUGH (N'land)   OS 77
The Lough lies 700 feet up in the Roman Wall country west of Hexham and on the direct route near the Tyne valley between the Solway and the east coast. It is the best of the Northumberland loughs in the area which includes Greenlee, Broomlee and Crag Loughs. Like most upland waters, Grindon is largely ignored by wildfowl with the exception of a herd of whooper swans that winter there. On passage, however, the Lough sometimes holds large numbers of duck for short periods and goosander and goldeneye have been quite numerous. An unusual development has been the increasing habit of a flock of bean geese to spend February in the neighbourhood.

WINTER: whooper—swan, goosander, goldeneye.
SPRING: bean goose, duck, curlew.
SUMMER: black-headed gull.

The Lough is private but can be viewed from the road to the south. Leave Hexham westwards on the A69 to Haydon Bridge. Turn right on the B6319 and immediately under the railway bridge turn left. After 2 miles turn left at a cross-roads and view the Lough on the right after 1 mile.

HURWORTH BURN (Durham)   OS 85
This is a small reservoir, less than half a mile long, 6 miles west of Hartlepool. It has a small duck population of the commoner species and there is usually a passage of waders, terns and, notably, little gulls, in autumn.

WINTER: wigeon, tufted duck, shoveler, whooper, swan.
AUTUMN: waders, terns, little gull.

Leave Hartlepool westwards on the A179 and continue on the B1280 when it joins the A19. After 1 mile turn left, fork right and turn right to the reservoir. A public footpath runs along the western side and must be strictly kept to.

LINDISFARNE (N'land)

OS 64 and 71; HT −0:46 River Tyne

Lindisfarne lies on the coast equidistant from Berwick and Alnwick and is a National Nature Reserve that will, when fully declared, exceed 6,000 acres. It will then cover the entire inter-tidal area between Budle Bay in the south and Cherwick Sands in the north, plus a separate area near Cheswick Black Rocks, as well as the large area of dunes on Holy Island and the mainland at Ross Links. The area includes a whole series of exceptionally fine bird habitats with Goswick Sands, Fenham Flats, Skate Road, Ross Links, Holy Island Lough and Budle Bay being the most outstanding.

The Reserve is being managed in the same way as the successful Caerlaverock Reserve in Dumfries with orderly shooting on a controlled basis. This will thus ease the position of Budle Bay which has been made untenable in the past by constant disturbance. Amongst the wildfowl the brent geese, 500–2,000, are the major interest. The majority of these are of the light-bellied or Atlantic race and large numbers usually only occur in the latter part of the winter. Pink-footed and greylag geese are also frequently present and whooper swans reach 450, the biggest herd in England. A few Bewick's also occur. On the open sea, especially off Skate Road, sea ducks are numerous. This area is also very good for grebes and divers though the concentration of 40 Slavonian, 27 red-necked, 9 great crested and 60 red-throated divers on one day in 1964 is probably exceptional.

Waders too are numerous with a variety of species present in flocks of several hundreds in autumn. Almost anything can and does turn up in the area, though barnacle geese in autumn are annual.

WINTER: brent, pink-footed and greylag geese, whooper, mute and Bewick's swans, wigeon, eider, scoter, goldeneye, long-tailed duck, Slavonian and red-necked grebes, divers, waders.

SPRING: waders.

AUTUMN: duck, barnacle goose, grey plover, bar-tailed godwit, little stint, whimbrel, wood sandpiper, spotted redshank, sanderling.

The whole of the reserve is of free public access though collecting specimens is by permit only and no mist-netting of birds is allowed. Access to farmland on Holy Island is not allowed,

Lindisfarne National Nature Reserve: showing the main access points and outstanding bird areas

and to that on the mainland only by permission of individual land owners. The most important access points from north to south are:

1. At Fenham near Mill Burn.
2. North of Fenham le-Moor at Lowmoor Point.
3. The road east of Beal and the causeway across to Holy Island.

4. North of Elwick to Whitelee Letch.

5. East of Ross a footpath leads across Ross Links to Ross Back Sands and Skate Road.

6. North-east of Budle.

7. North-west of Budle at Heather Cottages.

8. On Holy Island, the road leading north to The Links.

9. East of Holy Island to Sheldrake Pool.

The main A1 passes within a mile or two of all of these sites, some 14 miles north of Alnwick. See Map, page 95.

MARSDEN ROCKS (Durham)   OS 78

The Rocks lie between South Shields and Sunderland on a rather attractive cliff-backed stretch of coastline. Marsden Rock itself is a high, rugged stack separated from the mainland cliffs but joined by the sandy beach. Its ledges and flat top harbour nesting sea birds and the area is also well placed for sea-watching on a productive coast.

SUMMER: kittiwake, shag, cormorant, fulmar.

Leave South Shields southward on the coastal A183. At Marsden Bay a footpath leads along the cliff top to the Rocks.

SWALLOW PONDS (N'land)   OS 78

These ponds, which lie immediately north of Wallsend in the Tyneside conurbation, were formed by mining subsidence. In spite of the depressing surroundings which include pit heaps and a rubbish tip, the area is attractive to birds, including both wild swans in winter and a variety of fresh waders on passage. They are more properly and romantically called The Rising Sun Colliery subsidence pit and Wallsend rubbish dump.

WINTER: whooper and Bewick's swans, tufted duck.

SPRING AND AUTUMN: waders.

Leave Newcastle northwards on the A1 and after 2½ miles turn right at Gosforth on to the A191. Continue for 3 miles until this road merges with the A186 and then stop in half a mile where a track leads off to the right. Swallow Pond is on the right down this public right of way but is private and must be viewed from the footpath.

TEESMOUTH (Durham)
                          OS 85 and 86; HT at Middlesbrough

The estuary of the River Tees is virtually surrounded by industrial development, and abuts on to the Middlesbrough–Stockton conurbation. In spite of this the number of birds has increased in recent years and the area is one of the most important for waders in the north-east. Wildfowl are quite numerous on Seal Sands and many resort to the fleets and

dykes of the adjacent marshes. Waders use the same area and
a wide variety of species is found in winter and on passage.

Terns of five species frequently gather in the estuary in
August and skuas are sometimes quite numerous. The latter
are also noted offshore from South Gare at the estuary mouth,
together with sea duck, divers, gannets and other sea birds.

WINTER: wigeon, shelduck, scoter, whooper and Bewick's
swans, knot, bar-tailed godwit, golden and grey plovers,
sanderling.

SPRING: waders, duck.

SUMMER: waders, duck.

AUTUMN: godwits, whimbrel, ruff, spotted redshank, greenshank, sandpipers, grey plover, little stint, commic, roseate
and black terns, skuas, scoter, velvet scoter, gannet, fulmar,
kittiwake, eider.

Access details are changing very rapidly and anyone inter-
ested in watching in the area should contact Mrs. A. Cooper,
Honorary Secretary, Teesmouth Bird Club, 85 Junction Road,
Norton, Stockton-on-Tees. Mrs. Cooper is quite willing to help
and keeps up to date with the various arrangements with land-
owners and wildfowlers.

1. NORTH GARE BREAKWATER: can be reached by walking
along the beach from Seaton Carew or by walking across the
North Gare sands from a private road owned by the Tees
Conservancy Commissioners. This road may be closed in
the near future.

2. SEAL SANDS: can be viewed from North Gare Sands,
see 1.

3. SOUTH GARE BREAKWATER: access is by a private road
owned by Dorman Long (Steel) Ltd and the Tees Conservancy Commission, and public access may be limited in
future. The area can also be reached on foot from Redcar
along Coatham Sands.

TWEED ESTUARY (N'land)

OS 64; HT −0:58 River Tyne

The Tweed enters the sea 3 miles south of the Scottish border
between Berwick and Tweedmouth. Being both small and completely enclosed by urban development the area is not outstanding but does offer a variety of species, often at quite close
range. The tidal area stretches inland 2 miles to Yarrow Slake
though the best part is on the northern shore near the mouth.
Waders congregate on the sandy beach just north of the pier at
high tide.

WINTER: goldeneye, grebes, divers, waders.

SPRING: waders.

SUMMER: terns, mute swan.

AUTUMN: waders, sea birds.

The water front at Berwick east of the bridges is of straight-forward access leading out to the pier which is good for waders and sea bird passage.

Nottinghamshire

ATTENBOROUGH GRAVEL PITS   OS 112, 121

The pits lie in the Trent Valley just upstream from Nottingham and have been made a nature reserve. There are some areas of reed, and fairly thick vegetation of alder and willow flanks the River Trent. Wildfowl are quite plentiful and odd visitors include sawbills on the Trent. On passage common terns (which breed in the vicinity) and black terns are frequently noted, with small numbers of waders.

WINTER: wigeon, tufted duck, pochard, sawbills.

SPRING: waders, common and black terns.

SUMMER: sedge and reed warblers, wagtails, pochard, shoveler.

AUTUMN: common and black terns, sandpipers, greenshank.

Access is unrestricted. There are three possible entrances, all originating from the A453 west of Nottingham:

1. From Beeston Rylands to the Lock and then along the Trent.
2. From Chilwell Golf Course approach, take the Crescent at the end and follow the path eastwards to the river.
3. From Attenborough Station and south-east to the river.

CLUMBER PARK   OS 103 and 112

The Park lies 2½ miles south-east of Worksop and is the only one of the three large Dukeries lakes open to the public. The main attraction is the winter wildfowl and there is a great deal of movement between this lake and those at Welbeck and Thoresby. The Park also holds a variety of woodland species.

WINTER: shoveler, pochard, goldeneye, goosander, Canada goose, siskin, redpoll.

SUMMER: redstart, nightingale, warblers, goldcrest.

Leave Worksop westwards on the A57 and enter the Park at Manton Lodge on the right after 3 miles. Other points of access are A614, Apley Head Lodge, Normanton Gate and Drayton Gate; A6009 Carburton cross roads; A6009 Clumber Lane End.

The area is a favourite one for fishermen in winter and week-

day visits are advised if possible as the birds are then generally
less disturbed. The Park is owned by the National Trust.

HOVERINGHAM GRAVEL PITS   OS 112
Situated 10 miles north-east of Nottingham to the north of the
River Trent. A number of pits have been and are being excavated and a large area of open water has been created. Diving
ducks are as numerous as anywhere in the Trent Valley.
Waders on passage include a scattering of the commoner
species, and commic terns are regularly noted.

WINTER: pochard, tufted duck, goosander, goldeneye.

AUTUMN: waders, commic terns.

Leave Nottingham eastwards on the A612 to Lowdham. Turn
right and then left to Caythorpe an attractive road beside the
Trent. After a sharp corner leaving the river, turn right through
Hoveringham. As the road bends outside the village watch out
for a tiny stream and bridle path sign on right. Close gate
and walk along southern side of the best pits.

Shropshire
LONG MYND   OS 129
This is an extensive area of moorland in the south-west of the
county near the Welsh border. Its upland qualities give it a
bird population with closer affinities to that country than to
neighbouring England. The wooded valleys and streams hold
the usual species.

SUMMER: red grouse, ring ouzel, whinchat, grey wagtail,
dipper, pied flycatcher, wood warbler, redstart.

Leave Shrewsbury southwards on the A49 and turn right on
to the B4370 to Church Stretton. Carding Mill Valley is worth
exploring and the whole area is of generally unrestricted access.

NORTH SHROPSHIRE MERES   OS 118
These are a group of natural meres lying south and east of
Ellesmere to the north-west of Shrewsbury. The largest is the
lake at Ellesmere itself, covering 114 acres and extensively
used for boating. The resort aspect is intensified near the
church on the A528 where seats overlook the water and Canada
geese browse the roadside verge. Other waters include Cole
Mere, White Mere, Blake Mere, Crose Mere and Newton Mere.
They are extensively used by wildfowl, and a variety of
aquatic species, including black-necked grebe and roosting
gulls; great crested grebes breed on Ellesmere and Newton
Meres.

WINTER: wigeon, shoveler, pochard, goldeneye, goosander, Canada goose, cormorant, gulls.

SUMMER: great crested grebe, reed and sedge warblers.

AUTUMN: waders, black tern, commic tern, black-necked grebe.

1. ELLESMERE:adjacent to the A528 on the east side.

2. WHITE MERE: 1½ miles south of the A528.

3. COLE MERE: leave the A528 eastwards at the north end of White Mere and in 1 mile turn left in the village to a track along the south side of the mere.

4. BLAKE MERE: stop on the A528 at its junction with the A495 and walk along the canal towpath eastwards.

5. NEWTON MERE: leave the A528 on to the A495 and take the first right after 1 mile. This leads to the south side of the mere.

VENUS POOL   OS 118

This water lies 5 miles south-east of Shrewsbury, south of the A458 between Cross Houses and Cound. It is an important site for wildfowl, and waders are frequently noted on passage, with green sandpipers sometimes quite numerous.

WINTER: teal, wigeon, shoveler, tufted duck, pochard, shelduck, Canada goose.

SUMMER: tufted duck, mute swan, great crested grebe.

AUTUMN: ringed plover, green sandpiper, ruff.

Leave Shrewsbury southwards on the A458, half a mile past Cross Houses turn left towards Upper Cound, cross the railway and the Pool is on the left. Access is strictly on production of a membership card of the Shropshire Ornithological Society.

Somerset

AXE ESTUARY AND BREAN DOWN
OS 165; HT −0:05 Cardiff

The estuary forms the southern arm of Weston Bay and lies within 1 mile of Weston-super-Mare. The Axe Estuary attracts small numbers of waders, duck and gulls and is locally considered worth a look after Brean Down. This 300 foot limestone outcrop juts out 1 mile into the Bristol Channel and is cliff bound on the southern side. It is National Trust property and is maintained by Axbridge RDC. It is an ideal migration watch point and grounded passerines are sometimes numerous. Visible migration is heavy in October, and in winter odd sea duck occur offshore – rare for Somerset.

WINTER: sea duck, duck, knot, redshank, ringed plover.

SPRING: waders, migrants, chats, grasshopper warbler.

SUMMER: stonechat, raven, kestrel.

AUTUMN: warblers, chats, goldcrest, visible migrants, knot, ringed plover.

Leave Weston southwards on the A370 and turn right to Lympsham after 4½ miles. Half a mile after the village turn left and later right to Brean. Turn north to Brean Down. A path leads up to the top from the cafe and access is unrestricted. A path past Brean Down Farm leads out to the sea wall along the southern side of the Axe. There is a foot-ferry from Uphill for access to the area from Weston.

BLAGDON RESERVOIR   OS 165

Blagdon is some 10 miles south-west of Bristol on the northern side of the Mendip Hills. The water is 1½ miles by half a mile, and covers 430 acres. Though rather overshadowed by the Chew Valley Reservoir, 2 miles to the east, Blagdon is considerably older (1904), has its own attractions, and is still ranked as the seventh best reservoir for wildfowl. These include maxima of over a thousand each of wigeon, teal and pochard.

Waders are not as plentiful as at Chew, but autumn brings spotted redshank and sandpipers as well as black terns.

WINTER: wigeon, teal, shoveler, pochard, tufted duck, pintail, goldeneye, redpoll, siskin.

SPRING: waders, yellow wagtail.

AUTUMN: spotted redshank, greenshank, black tern.

Leave Bristol southwards on the A38 and turn left at Cowslip Green 1 mile past Redhill. After threequarters of a mile turn left and, after a similar distance, right to the dam from which views can be obtained. Entry is by permit only, details as at Chew.

BRIDGWATER BAY NATIONAL NATURE RESERVE
OS 165; HT at Cardiff

The Reserve consists of the Parrett Estuary, the Huntspill River and Stert Island, but for the purpose of this note areas outside the Reserve proper are included. The Reserve covers 6,076 acres, all which is of free access except Stert Island. Habitats include mud flats, shingle banks, salting and farmland, and the variety of birds is wide. Wildfowl are numerous and the area is a regular haunt of 1,500 white-fronts. It is unique as the British moulting ground for up to 3,000 shelduck in autumn, and 500 are present in winter.

Waders are numerous, especially in autumn, and large numbers flight up river at high tide. Merlins and short-eared owls are regularly present in winter.

WINTER: white-fronted goose, wigeon, pintail, shoveler, knot, turnstone, merlin, short-eared owl.
SPRING: whimbrel.
SUMMER: redshank, ringed plover, shelduck.
AUTUMN: shelduck, grey plover, whimbrel, godwits, knot, spotted redshank.
The area can be worked from two sides:

1. Leave Bridgwater westwards on the A39 and turn right at Cannington on to unclassified roads past Combwich to Steart. Walk northwards from here out towards Stert Point.
2. Leave Bridgwater northwards on the A38 to West Huntspill and follow the footpath along the Huntspill River out to the Island. Walk northwards for views over the flats and Stert Island.

High tide visits advised.

CHEW VALLEY RESERVOIR   OS 165
The reservoir lies some 8 miles south of Bristol and is 2 miles by over 1 mile. It was formed by damming the Chew River just east of Chew Stoke in 1953, and now covers 1,210 acres. The banks are mostly natural and there is a sizeable island in the north-eastern corner. The lake is the second most important reservoir for wildfowl in Britain. Surface feeders notably pintail and shoveler are dominant though both pochard and tufted duck have exceeded a thousand. Among the more exciting wildfowl, gadwall (100) in autumn, garganey in spring and summer, and smew are regular, and white-fronts are frequently present in small parties.

In spring and autumn Chew is outstanding for waders. Divers turn up occasionally in winter as do black-necked and Slavonian grebes, and great crested grebes usually breed in some numbers. Other species include the occasional little gull and a quite heavy double passage of black terns. In winter the lake is a sizeable gull roost and it is also the foremost trout lake in England.

WINTER: gadwall, wigeon, shoveler, pintail, pochard, goldeneye, smew, white-fronted goose, Bewick's swan, divers, waders, rock/water pipit.
SPRING: gadwall, garganey, waders, black tern, yellow wagtail.
SUMMER: gadwall, great crested grebe.
AUTUMN: gadwall, grey plover, jack snipe, godwits, green and wood sandpipers, spotted redshank, curlew sandpiper, ruff, black tern, migrants.

Leave Bristol southwards on the A38 and turn left after 5 miles on the B3130 to Chew Magna. Turn right before the village on the B3114 to Chew Stoke. Various cul de sacs lead to the reservoir surrounds but it can also be viewed from the public highway at Villice Bay, Heron Green, Herriott's Bridge and the dam. For regular visitors entry may be obtained by permit only available at a cost of 20s. per annum, or 10s. 6d. for juniors. This permit entitles the holder to visit all of the important Somerset reservoirs and is available from the Fisheries Officer, Bristol Waterworks Co., Woodford Lodge, Chew Stoke, Bristol. Day permits are available without charge on application (SAE).

EXMOOR
OS 163, 164

Exmoor lies within a rectangle with Lynmouth, South Molton, Dulverton and Minehead at its corners and consists of grass and heather moors with sheltered combes and deep-wooded valleys. Most of the moor is not common land though Withypool Common (1,866 acres) and Porlock Common (482 acres) are exceptions. The wooded valleys with their fast flowing streams are most attractive while higher up red grouse are found with black grouse in a few areas. Merlins usually try to breed.

SUMMER: buzzard, merlin, ring ouzel, dipper, grey wagtail, red and black grouse, pied flycatcher, wood and grasshopper warblers, nightjar.

Exmoor is not the place for a day out, and any bird-watching holiday should include exploration with the aid of OS maps. The area between Porlock and Dulverton is as good as any. Access to large areas is unrestricted, and many of the woodlands are open. Disturbance of the more unusual species should be avoided, and watchers particularly anxious to see black grouse and merlin are advised to look elsewhere. There are very few on Exmoor.

MINEHEAD–DUNSTER BEACHES
OS 164

The beaches immediately east of Minehead Golf Club and consist of sand, mud and shingle stretching almost a mile out into the Bristol Channel. They are backed by pebble and sand dunes, and by the Golf Course as far east as the mouth of the River Avill. Between this and the A39 is an area of open grassland. East of the Avill is a chalet estate and beyond that fields to the Blue Anchor. In winter duck and a small flock of white-fronts haunt the fields while the shore holds good numbers of waders including the occasional purple sandpiper.

WINTER: white-fronted goose, wigeon, shoveler, turnstone, sanderling, puple sandpiper, golden plover.

AUTUMN: waders, terns.

Leave Minehead eastwards along The Strand to the Golf Course. A footpath from here runs to the mouth of the Avill, and the shore and beach are open. A metalled road from Marsh Street, Dunster runs out to the shore east of the estate and there is a charge for use of the car park in summer. The white-fronts are easily visible from the beach path and must not be disturbed. High tide visits are advised.

PORLOCK MARSH   OS 164

The march is immediately behind the beach in Porlock Bay 6 miles west of Minehead. The area is mainly grazing land with pebble banks, gorse, a reed bed and some shallow pools. Duck are present in winter with small numbers of the commoner waders. On passage fresh waders are frequently present and more irregular visitors include bittern and the occasional rarity.

WINTER: wigeon, teal, shoveler, waders.

SPRING AND AUTUMN: whimbrel, sandpipers, greenshank, little stint, ruff.

Leave Porlock and the A39 by Sparkhayes Lane 100 yards north-east of the Church and continue on foot to the shore. Access, which is restricted to the beach and the footpath behind it, can also be obtained directly along the coast from Porlock Weir and Bossington Beach.

WET MOOR   OS 177

Wet Moor lies on the south side of the River Yeo, 7 miles north-west of Yeovil. Of all the Somerset Levels, this is the most reliable for winter flooding usually being 4 feet deep from mid-January to mid-February. During this period it is frequented by large numbers of dabbling duck as well as Bewick's swans. There are waders on passage in spring and autumn.

WINTER: (Jan–Feb): wigeon, pintail, shoveler, tufted duck, pochard, Bewick's swan, golden plover.

SPRING: black-tailed godwit.

SUMMER: redshank, curlew, corn bunting.

AUTUMN: greenshank, snipe, ruff.

Leave Langport eastwards on the A372 and turn south on the B3165 at Long Sutton. Stop at the bridge over the Yeo just before Long Load, where footpaths lead westwards along both banks. Several minor roads lead into the Moor from the Long Load–Muchelney Road.

Suffolk

BENACRE, COVEHITHE AND EASTON BROADS
OS 137

These coastal broads are similar and attract similar species of birds. Each is separated from the sea by only a narrow shingle beach and has a fairly large area of open water surrounded by a dense growth of reeds. Rough grazing meadows stretch inland from the broads. There are coverts of both deciduous and coniferous trees which, though strictly private, can provide interesting bird-watching from public footpaths.

Winter watching includes a good collection of duck and divers are sometimes present. Marsh harriers often fly up from Minsmere.

WINTER: teal, wigeon, goldeneye, smew.

SUMMER: sedge and reed warblers.

AUTUMN: terns, gulls, waders, marsh harrier.

Leave the A12 at Wrentham and turn eastwards to Covehithe, walk north to Benacre and south to Easton taking in the smaller Covehithe Broad on the way. Easton can also be approached northwards along the beach from Southwold via Easton Bavents, where quite recently built houses are tumbling into the sea. Sea watches from Covehithe cliffs are good.

BLYTH ESTUARY
OS 137; HT +0:35 Lowestoft at Southwold

The estuary is directly east of the A12 at Blythburgh, which is 10 miles north of Saxmundham. The River Blyth formerly ran between high banks with water meadows on either side but floods in 1921 and 1926 broke the walls and a large area became tidal. Recent attempts to reclaim the north-western section have been unsuccessful but have allowed some emergent vegetation to flourish, improving its attraction for certain species. Parts of the old embankments still exist and excellent views of the estuary can be obtained from these. They serve as roosts for waders and gulls.

The main attraction is the number of waders and black-tailed godwits are particularly numerous in spring, often reaching 300. Autumn passage is good and several hundred duck are present in winter. Gadwall and spotted redshank in winter are specialities. There is considerable movemen to Walberswick marshes at high tide.

WINTER: spotted redshank, wigeon, shelduck.

The Blyth Estuary: a notable haunt of black-tailed godwit and spotted redshank

SPRING: black-tailed godwit, bar-tailed godwit, grey plover, whimbrel.

SUMMER: redshank, common tern, shelduck.

AUTUMN: spotted redshank, little stint, knot, grey plover, whimbrel.

Good views can be obtained from the roadside embankment a quarter of a mile north of Blythburgh on the A12. Further views can be obtained by walking eastwards along a footpath starting at a row of cottages near the inn. This is an old railway track and surrounding land is private.

Southwold is an ideal centre but Blythburgh has a good inn with views over the estuary.

HAVERGATE ISLAND   OS 150

Havergate is situated in the estuary of the Ore and is only separated from the sea by the shingle spit of Orfordness. Two miles downstream from Orford, the island covers 280 acres of former water meadows that through wartime neglect and subsequent management have been converted into a wonderful wader marsh. Almost the entire island lies below high water mark and newly constructed sluices enable the water level to be carefully controlled to attract the maximum number of species. The RSPB was quick to acquire the island when avocets were found so that its other attractions tend to be unnoticed. Winter brings a very large wildfowl population amongst which pintail and Bewick's swans are notable.

WINTER: pintail, shoveler, wigeon, Bewick's swan, knot, grey plover, short-eared owl, merlin, hen harrier.

SPRING: godwits, whimbrel, turnstone.

SUMMER: avocet, common and Sandwich terns, short-eared owls.

AUTUMN: godwits, ruff, greenshank, green, wood and curlew sandpipers, little stint.

Access to the island is by boat from Orford Quay, escorted by the Warden. Permits (15s. per day), must be booked in advance from the RSPB and are limited to twelve on any one day. The reserve is not open every day and intending visitors should consult the Society well in advance.

MINSMERE   OS 137

Minsmere is situated on the coast about 2 miles south of Dunwich. It is one of the most important reserves of the RSPB and covers 1,500 acres of marsh, lagoon, reed, heath and woodland. From the point of view of the number of species seen it is probably the best place in Britain for a day's bird-watching. In many ways it is similar to the Walberswick area to the north but has been considerably improved to attract and leave undisturbed a great variety of unusual birds. The coastal dune system protects large lagoons with islands known as 'The Scrape' that harbour breeding avocets and terns and swarm with waders in spring and autumn. Westwards there is an extensive reed bed with large patches of open water, providing a habitat for duck and the regular spoonbill. The woodland is a delightful area and contains most of the song birds one could expect to see in southern England, while the heath is excellent and stone curlew breed on the specially prepared fields. There are several well sited hides giving undisturbed views over the most interesting areas.

WINTER: Bewick's swan, hen harrier, marsh harrier, waders.

SPRING: whimbrel, spotted redshank.

SUMMER: avocet, marsh harrier, common and Sandwich terns, bearded tit, stone curlew, red-backed shrike, nightingale, sedge and reed warblers, corn bunting.

AUTUMN: spotted redshank, little stint, curlew sandpiper, black tern, spoonbill, great grey shrike.

Access is by permit in advance only. These are available at a price of 15s. escorted and 10s. unescorted on various days of

the week. Full details for the current year are available from
the RSPB.

The reserve is approached along a road leaving the Dunwich–
Westleton road to the south, threequarters of a mile from Dunwich. This runs into a rough track after 1¼ miles when a small
toll may have to be paid. Continue past the Coastguard Cottages to the hill overlooking the reserve. At this point a good
look at the sea is often fruitful. A flock of red-throated divers
is frequently present in winter.

Continue on foot southward between the sea walls until a
gate with a notice on the right invites your entry, if a permit
holder. For non-permit holders a public shore hide to the south
of the official entrance gives excellent views of the pools and
avocets.

STOUR ESTUARY   OS 150; HT +0:40 Harwich
The estuary lies on the Essex border and provides not only the
largest expanse of tidal water but also the primary resort of
wildfowl in Suffolk. Being rather shallow, diving duck are
scarce but wigeon and shelduck are particularly numerous
on the huge mudbanks on both shores. Wigeon frequently
number 4,000 and have reached 13,700. Both species of godwit
winter, and the black-tailed builds up to sizeable flocks in
spring. The concentration of mute swans, up to 900, at the
malthouses at Mistley in autumn is notable.

WINTER: wigeon, pintail, shelduck, brent goose, godwits,
grey plover.
SPRING: black-tailed godwit, turnstone.
AUTUMN: waders, mute swan.

There are four basic approaches to the Stour, all start from
Manningtree Station on the A137, 10 miles south of Ipswich
and north of Colchester.

On the Essex shore:

1. Take the road to Manningtree from the station and continue, joining the B1352 to Mistley to see the autumn gathering of mute swans.

2. Continue through Bradfield and take the second turning left after 2 miles. There is an inn on the corner. This road
passes under the railway and a track leaves to the left after
200 yards to Jacques Bay. Return to and continue along
the metalled road to Wrabness Halt where a track leads off
to the left for views over Copperas Bay.

3. The section from Copperas to Harwich is the primary
haunt of brent geese and is viewed from the Parkston Quay
area.

On the Suffolk shore:

4. Leave Manningtree station by the A137 northwards keep right after 3 miles on the B1080 to Stutton. Turn right and then left to the church. Continue past the church to Holbrook Bay. Returning, turn right past the church to the B1080 then turn right to Holbrook. Turn right past the church and continue to Harkstead in 2 miles. Turn right down to Holbrook Bay.

WALBERSWICK   OS 137

Situated on the coast 1 mile south of Southwold, Walberswick has a variety of habitat that makes it a good centre. The dune beach protects an area of low lying ground that extends inland for some 2½ miles and which is drained by the Dunwich River. The area clearly shows the effects of various degrees of salinity and the principal habitats may be classified as follows: a series of shallow brackish pools behind the sea wall, exposing considerable areas of mud; a huge reed bed with a few open lagoons, which gives way to rough grass and thorn and birch scrub; the final habitat is the dry heathland which is being invaded by birch scrub and which is dotted with old pine and

Walberswick: walk southward along the shore from the car park and be careful about taking the correct wall. Left at the Wind pump to Hoist Covert and the heath beyond. Stick strictly to paths and avoid offending local landowners

mixed coverts. The Dingle Hills were formerly a rabbit-warren but myxamotosis decimated the rabbits and gorse has grown largely unchecked. The hills are used by the Dingle Bird Club as a bird observatory and ringing station.

Specialities of the area include a large range of breeding birds. In spring and autumn wader passage is often excellent and the Dingle Hills are worth a look for passerines. Winter brings fair numbers of duck, regular hen harriers and good numbers of snow buntings.

Most of the area is private land and visitors must keep strictly to the rights of way and paths where the various land-owners have given general permission to walk. The coverts and heath in particular are sacrosanct, not only because of the breeding birds but because they are preserved as shooting, and well-keepered shooting at that.

WINTER: gadwall, hen harrier, short-eared owl, snow bunting, twite, waders.

SPRING: whimbrel, sanderling.

SUMMER: sedge, reed and grasshopper warblers, red-backed shrike, terns, scoter.

AUTUMN: ruff, little stint, curlew sandpiper, marsh harrier, snow bunting, twite, shore lark.

Leaving the A12 1 mile south of Blythburgh, turn eastwards on to the B387 and continue on to the B1387 after 1 mile. Leave the village southwards along the beach. Take the second wall past this area to the windpump. Head past the windpump towards Hoist Covert, watching out for warblers, and on leaving the marsh, look out for red-backed shrike, and rarities in the bushes. Arriving at a road turn right to the village past collared doves in some well fir-treed gardens. The most interesting species can be seen from this route.

Surrey

FRENSHAM COMMON AND PONDS　　　　　OS 169

The common lies on either side of the A287 roughly half way between Farnham and Hindhead and covers 650 acres of heather with Scots pine. The area is a rough, sandy waste with numerous hills giving wide views over the surrounding countryside. Birch scrub and plantations of deciduous trees are more numerous in the eastern part beyond the Little Pond. The two ponds are not particularly exciting from a wildfowl point of view but in summer the whole area is alive with small passerines. In particular the area of pines, birches and scrub near the main road on the Little Pond side is excellent. Buzzards now breed in the vicinity and can occasionally be seen soaring.

SUMMER: stonechat, woodlark, nightjar, warblers, wood warbler, lesser white-throat, redstart, nightingale, goldcrest, buzzard.

WINTER: siskin, redpoll, great grey shrike, wildfowl.

Leave the A287 at the Great Pond car park on the northern side. The whole area can be explored by the numerous tracks.

THURSLEY AND OCKLEY COMMONS   OS 169

The two commons are to the west of the A3, between Milford and Hindhead. The large area (893 acres) has a variety of habitats from wet bog, through grass, heather, birch scrub, to mature woodland and fir plantations. Apart from its value as a winter haunt of great grey shrike, it has a large variety of breeding species.

WINTER: great grey shrike.

SUMMER: redshank, curlew, snipe, tufted duck, woodlark grasshopper warbler, nightingale, redstart.

Leave the A3 westwards at Milford on the B3001 to Elstead. Turn left and park near Hammer Pond on the left. Gumboots are essential if one is to explore in all directions. The area is now a reserve of the Surrey NT.

Sussex

AMBERLEY WILD BROOKS   OS 182

Situated in the Arun valley near Arundel and together with the levels between Pulborough and Greatham form the most important area for wildfowl in Sussex. The new year is the best time. Wigeon sometimes exceed 4,000, white-fronts, pink-feet and greylags have all been noted, and Bewick's swans are becoming regular.

WINTER: wigeon, teal, pintail, shoveler, pochard, mute and Bewick's swans.

Leave A29 6 miles south of Pulborough at its junction with A284. Take the B2139 to Amberley. In the village and round to the east are several tracks leading to the Wild Brooks.

CHICHESTER GRAVEL PITS   OS 181

There are two main groups of pits north-east and south-east of Chichester, within 4 miles of the sea. Dabbling duck are dominant in autumn and as their number declines with winter so the number of diving duck increase to a peak of several hundred.

During passage periods terns and gulls are numerous with black tern regular, but the ornithology of the pit is dominated by the huge passage of hirundines that use the area as a major staging roost. Over 6,000 sand martins are ringed annually by a group formed to take advantage of the concentration.

WINTER: gadwall, pochard, tufted duck, scaup, great crested grebe.

AUTUMN: teal, sand martin, swallow, sedge and reed warblers.

The A27 round the east and south sides of Chichester passes most of the pits, but at the southern roundabout with the A259 take an obscure unclassified road to Runcton and fork left among the pits. Most can be viewed from the roads and open tracks.

CHICHESTER HARBOUR OS 181; HT +0:15 Portsmouth
The Harbour lies on the Hants–Sussex border and is closely related to Langstone and Portsmouth Harbours which lie in Hampshire. Records for Chichester are published on both county reports though the bulk of the area lies in Sussex. Wildfowl are quite numerous in winter with dark-bellied brent geese (up to 500) the main attraction. Waders are numerous and the usual population includes both godwits (bar-tailed more numerous). In spring numbers increase, while the huge autumn numbers reach a peak in September. The occasional ruff is found in winter and Black Point is a favourite winter haunt of the occasional little stint.

Divers are present in winter and both black-necked and Slavonian grebes are regular.

WINTER: brent goose, wigeon, shelduck, eider, merganser, grey plover, turnstone, knot, godwits, sanderling, divers, grebes.

SPRING: whimbrel, turnstone, godwits, sanderling.

AUTUMN: waders, green sandpiper, spotted redshank, greenshank, curlew sandpiper, little stint, godwits, grey plover, turnstone.

In Hampshire:

1. Leave the A27 at Havant southwards on the B2149 to Hayling Island. At Hayling Bay turn left along the coast to Black Point for excellent views of the mouth.

In Sussex:

2. Leave Chichester southwards on the A286 and after 1½ miles turn right to Dell Quay.

3. Continue on A286 past Manhood End, once a splendid place now a marina, and turn right to West Itchenor. Though a sailing resort a walk westwards along the harbour shore

gives good views towards Thorney Island after a half mile.
4. Continue on A286 to West Wittering where a 4s. 0d.
car park is established in summer. Walk along the foreshore
to East Head.

LANGNEY POINT AND THE CRUMBLES OS 183

This spot consists of a shingle peninsula similar to Dungeness
and a few quite small pits immediately east of Eastbourne. The
point is good for sea-watching and has produced a string of
rare and extremely rare birds. Perhaps the sewage outfall here
adds attraction to an already well-sited area. Scoter and skuas
and divers are regularly seen but terns and gulls are dominant.
Mediterranean gull, black and roseate terns are noted most
years. Chats are numerous on the shingle on passage and warblers shelter in the few patches of cover, amongst the dense
undergrowth in the area between Eastbourne and the new
estate, and at the Crumbles.

SPRING: divers, skuas, gulls, terns, roseate tern, chats.

AUTUMN: skuas, gulls, Mediterranean gull, terns, black tern,
chats, warblers, rarities.

Leave Eastbourne north-eastwards on the A259 but after
passing a park on the left watch for Vine Square on the right.
Turn into the square and continue on to Wartling Street. At
the point the flying of red flags marks the range area out of
bounds. Signs show the whereabouts of the sewage outfall.

Eastwards on the A259 Wallis Avenue runs through a new
housing estate out to the point. Further eastward take the
B2191 at a roundabout and turn right off the road immediately
past King's Caravan Site for the Crumbles.

THE MIDRIPS AND THE WICKS OS 184

Situated on the Kent boundary on the western side of the peninsula that terminates at Dungeness. A series of shallow pools
lie immediately behind the high shingle beach, being flooded
by sea water passing through the beach at high tides. Though
the water level has always been variable recent improvements
to the sea wall may alter the attractiveness of the area. Snow
buntings feed on the beach in winter and short-eared owls hunt
the rough ground.

During passage periods, gulls, terns and skuas are regularly
noted offshore. Waders are numerous and the more interesting
species are frequently present. Rarities have a habit of turning
up here.

WINTER: wigeon, pintail, shoveler, snow bunting, short-eared
owl.

SPRING AND AUTUMN: terns, gulls, skuas, waders.

Leave Rye eastwards on the A259 and turn right after 1 mile at Guldeford. Pass Camber and where the road leaves the coast park on the left. Walk up a track past some houses on to the sea wall and continue eastwards. If a red flag is flying the Lydd ranges are in use and access is forbidden.

PAGHAM HARBOUR   OS 181; HT −0:01 Portsmouth

The harbour is on the eastern side of the peninsula that ends in Selsey Bill and has been a nature reserve since 1964. Though the harbour was reclaimed in 1876 the sea regained control in 1910 since when the area of approximately 1 square mile has been one of the most notable bird haunts in the county. Wildfowl are never very numerous but include brent geese. Winter waders include both godwits and the pools at Sidlesham are extremely productive during migration.

WINTER: brent goose, eider, merganser, scoter, grey plover, turnstone, godwits, sanderling.

SPRING: whimbrel, turnstone, ringed plover.

SUMMER: little tern, ringed plover.

AUTUMN: whimbrel, wood sandpiper, spotted redshank, greenshank, knot, little stint, ruff, warblers, chats, short-eared owl.

Pagham Harbour: a local nature reserve and interesting bird resort at all seasons

Leave Chichester southwards on the B2145 or B2201 to Sidlesham:

1. The pools at Ferry Ho. Sidlesham are worth investigating, and paths run along the eastern side of the main pool, and along the south side of the harbour.
2. Continue to Church Norton and view harbour and sea.
3. Leave Chichester on the B2145 but turn left after 1 mile on to the B2166. After 2 miles turn right to Pagham. Continue right, past the church. A track leads to the right to the harbour wall. Turn left out along the shore line to the sea and Pagham Lagoon, the large water between the caravan site and the sea.

SELSEY BILL   O S 181

Selsey Bill is at the extreme south-western tip of the county and was the site of a bird observatory until bungalow development occupied the area. In spite of this, the Bill retains its attraction as a site for sea-watching. Passerines still occur and can be watched flitting through back-garden fences.

In winter divers and sea duck are sometimes numerous, and skuas, terns and fulmars are noted in April. Shearwaters join these species on the return passage, and visible migration is heavy in October.

WINTER: red-throated diver, merganser, scoter.
SPRING: divers, terns, skuas, fulmar, passerines, gull-billed tern, rarities.
SUMMER: collared dove.
AUTUMN: terns, skuas, pomarine skua, fulmar, Mank shearwater, Mediterranean gull, passerines, visible migrants.

Leave Chichester southward on the B2201 or B2145 and continue to the sea at Selsey Bill. The path eastward along the shore is best.

West Midlands (Staffordshire, Warwickshire and Worcestershire)

BELVIDE RESERVOIR (Stafford)   OS 119

This water lies north of Wolverhampton alongside the A5. It is a natural banked reservoir set among low lying agricultural land. There are large numbers of common duck as well as smew in late winter. The water collects the odd rare grebe and diver, and wader passage is regular. Black and commic terns are frequent and occasionally numerous.

WINTER: wigeon, shoveler, pochard, goldeneye, goosander, smew, Canada goose, snipe.

SPRING: waders, black and commic terns, garganey.

SUMMER: redshank, yellow wagtail.

AUTUMN: whimbrel, green sandpiper, greenshank, ruff, black and commic terns, garganey.

Leave Cannock westwards on the A5. The reservoir is to the south after 6 miles and can be seen from the road and from a track at the western end. Permits can be obtained from the West Midland Bird Club.

BLITHFIELD RESERVOIR (Stafford)   OS 120

This is an 800 acre water, 2½ miles by half a mile, between Rugeley and Uttoxeter. It was flooded in 1952 and is now ranked third amongst English reservoirs. Teal and wigeon both have peaks over 1,000, and pochard and tufted over 500. Shoveler, goosander and Canada goose all reach three figures, and flocks of goldeneye are quite large. Great crested grebes are numerous and the rarer grebes and divers turn up regularly.

Wader passage is the best in the West Midland area and black terns are present on both passages along with commic terns, and little gulls in autumn.

WINTER: wigeon, pochard, shoveler, goosander, goldeneye, pintail, Canada goose, Bewick's swan, great crested grebe, snipe, jack snipe.

SPRING: waders, black and commic terns.

AUTUMN: little ringed plover, turnstone, whimbrel, sandpipers, spotted redshank, little stint, curlew sandpiper, ruff, black and commic terns, little gull.

Leave Rugeley northwards on the B5013 to the reservoir causeway in 4 miles. A road southwards on the east side gives good views but only early in the morning because of light conditions.

CANNOCK CHASE (Stafford)   OS 119 and 120

This is a large stretch of infertile sandy heath, covering 25 square miles between Stafford, Rugeley and Cannock. Its natural vegetation is largely heather and bracken, though large areas have been planted with conifers by the Forestry Commission. Typical heathland and woodland birds breed freely and a few red grouse still survive. The area is partly common land and partly privately owned, and is the best in the West Midlands for oddities like harriers and shrikes.

WINTER: redpoll, siskin, stonechat.

SUMMER: nightjar, whinchat, redstart, wood and grasshopper warblers, long-eared owl, red grouse.

Within such a large area cover is generally inadequate and

watchers are urged to explore unknown sites. For a casual visit the area in the west around Brocton Field and Anson's Bank is very rewarding with special interest along the Sherbrook Valley, though Brownhills Common in the south is conveniently near the urban areas.

COOMBS VALLEY, LEEK (Stafford)   OS 111
An RSPB reserve covers 191 acres of this beautiful valley. The Coombs Brook is a swift flowing, boulder strewn stream beloved by dippers, and is flanked on both sides by stands of mixed woodland. There are also some areas of open bracken heath with birches. Breeding birds include black grouse, little owl and sparrow hawk.

SUMMER: sparrow hawk, little owl, dipper, kingfisher, grey wagtail, red and black grouse, woodcock, wheatear, stonechat, whinchat, redstart.

Access is by permit available with full details for the current season from the RSPB.

WYRE FOREST (Worcester)   OS 130
The forest is placed 5 miles west of Kidderminster and is 3 miles by 2 miles. It is an old forest of predominantly deciduous species but with an interesting sprinkling of conifers. It is bisected by a railway which runs alongside the attractive Dowles Brook.

SUMMER: kingfisher, redstart, pied flycatcher, tree pipit, wood warbler, warblers.

Leave Kidderminster westwards on the A456 and turn right at Bewdley on to the B4194. In 2½ miles stop at Buttonoak and explore southwards on footpaths.

Wiltshire

BY BROOK   OS 156
This beautiful stream runs through a deep, wooded valley for several miles but is at its best on either side of Castle Combe, voted the most beautiful village in England, north of the A420, 5 miles west of Chippenham.

A wide variety of woodland species breed.

SUMMER: dipper, grey wagtail, redstart, wood warbler.

Leave Chippenham westwards on the A420. Fork right on to the B4039 after 2½ miles and in 3 miles turn left at Castle Combe. Cross the bridge and walk north or south along the river.

LONGLEAT LAKE AND SHEARWATER   OS 166

Longleat Lake is set in the grounds of the mansion of that
name, one of the finest Elizabethan houses in Britain with
grounds by 'Capability' Brown, and is really a chain of lakes,
the largest being half a mile long. Shearwater is a larger lake,
lying 3 miles to the west and separated from Longleat by an
extensive area of woodland. Wildfowl of a fair variety are
present and there is usually a good collection of winter finches.
    WINTER: teal, shoveler, pochard, tufted duck, redpoll,
    siskin.
    SUMMER: buzzard, sparrowhawk, redstart, wood warbler.
    Leave Frome southwards on the B3092 and after 4 miles
turn left towards Horningsham. Longleat is on the left in $1\frac{1}{4}$
miles, and is open to the public daily, except on Christmas
Day. On leaving take the right fork of the two lanes opposite
and in $1\frac{1}{4}$ miles turn left. After 2 miles fork left and in $1\frac{1}{4}$ miles
view Shearwater on the left.

MARLBOROUGH DOWNS   OS 157

This area is to the north-west of Marlborough, and covers 25
square miles of high chalk downland. There is no common land
though access is frequently unrestricted. The area is full of
old field systems, earthworks, etc., and the wide horizons are
interrupted by the occasional clump of trees. Like Salisbury
Plain, its birds are rare and no one is going to publish details
of where to find what. In autumn harriers and golden plover
enliven the scene.
    SUMMER: buzzard, hobby, stone curlew, quail, wheatear.
    AUTUMN: buzzard, harriers, golden plover.
    Explore with OS map. The casual visitor motoring over the
top from Marlborough to Broad Hinton might well see something.

SALISBURY PLAIN   OS 167

Salisbury Plain is roughly enclosed by a line drawn from
Amesbury west to Deptford, to Warminster, to Westbury,
east to Market Lavington, and on to Upavon. The area is
chalk downland interrupted by belts and clumps of trees. There
are very few roads and most of the area west of the Shrewton–
West Lavington road is occupied by the military and to all
intents closed. The Plain has long been known as the breeding
haunt of a number of scarce birds. The first weekend in June
sees the egg collectors clambering around the copses after
hobby's eggs – against the law but still much practised.
    SUMMER: hobby, buzzard, stone curlew, quail, wheatear.

The A360 between Shrewton and West Lavington is good and so is the minor road to the east.

SAVERNAKE FOREST OS 157

Savernake lies south-east of Marlborough between the A4 and A346 and is the remnant of a royal deer forest. Its old oaks and beeches with their clearings can only be appreciated on foot. Though famous for fungi its birds include a variety of woodland species.

SUMMER: nightjar, redstart, nightingale, wood warbler.

Leave Marlborough on either the A4 or A346 south-eastwards and explore numerous tracks and paths.

Yorkshire

BEMPTON CLIFFS OS 93

These cliffs lie immediately north of Flamborough Head and rise higher (450 feet). They have been noted for many years as the only mainland breeding site of the gannet in Britain and 6 pairs now breed. They are, however, easy to miss amongst the vast numbers of kittiwakes (possibly 40,000 pairs between Flamborough and Bempton). Rock doves, indistinguishable from pure wild stock, breed.

SUMMER: gannet, kittiwake, guillemot, razorbill, puffin, fulmar, rock dove.

Leave Bridlington eastwards on the B1255 and turn left in Flamborough to Bempton. It is possible to drive right out to the cliffs. There is a footpath along the cliff tops from Flamborough Head.

DERWENT FLOODS OS 98

In the Derwent Valley between Wheldrake and Bubwith, 6 miles north-east of Selby. The floods usually last for 6–8 weeks in February–March and then hold a huge population of several thousand wildfowl, including up to 100 Bewick's swans. Whooper swans and geese are sometimes seen.

WINTER: wigeon, teal, pintail, shoveler, pochard, goldeneye, Bewick's swan.

Leave Selby northwards on the A19 and turn right 1 mile past Barlby on to the A163. Continue to Bubwith and inspect the river northwards just before the village. In 1 mile turn left on the B1228. Most of the area can be seen from this and minor roads leading to Aughton, Elerton, East Cottingwith and Storwood. Try Aughton churchyard.

ECCUP RESERVOIR AND HAREWOOD PARK LAKE
OS 96

Situated 5–8 miles north of Leeds to the west of the A61, Eccup
is just over a mile long, has natural banks and a mixed winter
population of duck, including goosander, which reach a maximum in March. Harewood Lake is set in mixed woodland and
has a large flock (once 750) of Canada geese. Black tern,
waders, etc., turn up mainly in autumn in small numbers.

WINTER: wigeon, shoveler, tufted duck, smew, goosander,
Canada goose, Bewick's swan.

AUTUMN: waders, terns.

Access to both places is by permits which are only issued to
members of the Leeds and District Bird Watchers Club.
Membership which costs 20s. is limited to 80. All inquiries
to the Honorary Secretary, c/o The City Museum, Leeds.

FAIRBURN INGS   OS 97
The Aire subsidences are a series of marshes up to 600 yards
wide between Swillington and Newton, and form one of the
most important wetlands in England, in spite of considerable
disturbance from industrial activities. The area at Fairburn
has been declared a local nature reserve. Duck, many of which
breed, are numerous and both wild swans occur regularly.
Passage brings waders, black terns, water rails and in early
September, the number of sand martins and swallows coming
to roost has been estimated at well over a million birds.

WINTER: wigeon, shoveler, pochard, goldeneye, gadwall,
Bewick's and whooper swans.

SPRING: garganey.

SUMMER: sedge and reed warblers, shoveler, pochard, gadwall.

AUTUMN: sand martin, swallow, black tern, water rail,
waders, garganey.

Leave the A1 westwards at Fairburn, 2 miles north of Ferry-
bridge. This road runs along the northern side of the reserve,
and there is a footpath across the marsh along a raised wall.
Access otherwise is by permit obtainable from R. F. Dickens,
Ridgefield, Glasshoughton Hill, Castleford, W. Riding, Yorks.
Enclose s.a.e.

FLAMBOROUGH HEAD   OS 93
The Head is the largest projection from what is otherwise a
generally smooth coastline. The chalk cliffs rise to 250 feet
and provide nesting sites for large numbers of kittiwakes and a
fine vantage point for observing sea birds, including unusual

species. Passerines, including warblers, chats and fly-catchers, are regular and occasionally large falls occur.

SPRING: divers, fulmars, terns, auks.

SUMMER: kittiwake, scoter.

AUTUMN: divers, fulmar, Manx and sooty shearwaters, gannet, skuas, terns, auks, passerines.

Leave Bridlington eastwards on the B1255. Continue straight on the B1259 at Flamborough and drive to the Head.

HORNSEA MERE   OS 99

Lying less than a mile from the sea behind the village of Hornsea, the mere covers 300 acres, and has extensive areas of reed-bed. Hornsea would be a good haunt anywhere in Britain but its geographical position makes it quite outstanding. Large numbers of wildfowl winter and wild swans are regularly present. Passage can bring almost anything to the area but bittern, black tern, little gull, Slavonian grebe and a number of sea birds are all annual visitors.

WINTER: wigeon, shoveler, pochard, goldeneye goosander, Bewick's and whooper swans.

SPRING: black tern, garganey, bittern.

SUMMER: pochard, tufted duck, shoveler, heron, warblers.

AUTUMN: Slavonian grebe, water rail, waders, black tern, little gull, gannet.

A road signposted 'To the Mere' leads westwards out to a peninsula from Hornsea, car park, etc. The B1244 along the northern side gives good views at several points.

HUMBER WILDFOWL REFUGE

OS 98; HT +0:39 Hull

The refuge stretches 4 miles downstream from where the Rivers Trent and Ouse open out into a tidal estuary with shoals, saltings and an island. The area covers 3,130 acres between Faxfleet and Brough which are strictly preserved and wardened. The main species protected is the pink-foot of which 10,000 are usually present in early autumn with smaller numbers in winter. The birds roost on Whitton Sand and flight out to feed in the surrounding countryside. Other species include thousands of duck and small numbers of waders.

WINTER: pink-footed goose, wigeon, teal, shoveler, shelduck, waders.

AUTUMN: pink-footed goose.

Do not trespass on the reserve. The birds are best seen flighting in from several vantage points:

1. FAXFLEET: leave A63 1 mile west of Newport and drive southwards 4 miles to the estuary.

2. WHITTON: leave the A1077 6 miles west of South
Ferriby. 2 miles past South Ferriby view the estuary out towards Read's Island.

MALHAM TARN FIELD CENTRE   OS 90

Though better known to geologists than ornithologists, Malham
Tarn and the surrounding moorland and rough pasture provides an ideal base for getting to know the commoner moorland birds. Lying immediately north of the Aire–Ribble gap
Malham is easy to reach via the A65. Both peregrine and merlin
have bred in recent years, and over 140 species have been
recorded,

SUMMER: redstart, wheatear, ring ouzel, dipper, common
sandpiper, redshank, curlew, golden plover, red grouse,
peregrine, merlin, black-headed gull.

A general exploration of the area is advised with the Field
Centre serving as base. An excellent round trip involves a train
to Horton-in-Ribblesdale, climbing Pen-y-ghent direct and
turning south over Fountain's Fell down past the Tarn to the
Cove and Malham. The whole is energetic and should not be
undertaken without some experience of mountains. Mists can
come down very suddenly here.

Field Centre: details from Field Studies Council, 9 Devereux
Court, Strand, London WC2.

SPURN BIRD OBSERVATORY
OS 105; HT −0:10 Grimsby

The observatory lies at the south-eastern corner of the
county at the mouth of the Humber. It is a 3 mile long peninsula little more than 250 yards wide and is a nature reserve
of the Yorkshire NT. In winter the huge flats along the western
side of the Spurn are a notable haunt of waders and wildfowl.

Migrants include a large range of diurnal species coasting
in both spring and autumn, and terns, skuas, divers and waders
are present in good variety. Migrant chats, warblers and flycatchers are often involved in 'falls' in autumn, and there are
always a few rarities each season including regular great grey
shrike, barred and yellow-browed warblers and bluethroat.

WINTER: wigeon, teal, knot, redshank.
SPRING: divers, bar-tailed godwit.
SUMMER: little tern, ringed plover.
AUTUMN: spotted redshank, bar-tailed godwit, wood sandpiper, greenshank, curlew sandpiper, divers, terns, skuas,
chats, warblers, flycatchers, great shrike, barred and
yellow-browed warblers, bluethroat, rarities.

Leave Hull eastwards on A1033 and fork right in Patrington on the B1445 to Easington. Continue on unclassified roads to Kilnsea, and then south to Spurn. The reserve is private and there is an admission fee, there is also a public footpath. Accommodation at the Observatory is 5s. 0d. per night (4s. 0d. to Yorkshire NU members) for simple hostel arrangements. There is a resident warden with whom bookings should be made: Spurn Observatory, Kilnsea, via Patrington, Hull, E. Yorks.

WASHBURN VALLEY AND RESERVOIRS   OS 96

The valley is a tributary of the Wharfe and lies 12 miles north of Leeds. Three natural banked reservoirs have been created by damming the river and a fairly large area of the surrounding hillsides has been afforested.

WINTER: wigeon, pochard, goldeneye, whooper swan.

SUMMER: curlew, redshank, snipe, pied flycatcher, warblers.

Leave Otley northwards on unclassified roads to Newall. Turn right over the bridge on the B6451 and then left still on B6451 outside Farnley Hall. At Farnley continue to Lindley Bridge.

There are many footpaths in the valley, including one on the north side of Lindley Wood Reservoir, and on the south side of Swinsty Reservoir.

Permits for the reservoirs can be obtained from the General Manager and Engineer, Leeds Waterworks Dept., 182 Otley Road, West Park, Leeds 16.

Part 2: Wales

Anglesey

CEMLYN BAY   OS 106

The bay is on the north coast of Anglesey and consists of a brackish lagoon separated from the sea by a shingle bar, the sheltered bay, the rocky and weedy shore, and some wet pasture fields. The whole area is attractive to birds, in spite of the construction of the nuclear power station on nearby Wylfa Head, and is owned and managed as a bird sanctuary by the National Trust.

WINTER: wigeon, shoveler, pochard, goldeneye, whooper swan, turnstone, grey plover, redshank, bar-tailed godwit, golden plover.

SPRING and AUTUMN: waders.

Leave the A5025 1 mile west of Cemaes Bay at Tregele westwards to Cemlyn. Past Plas Cemlyn a signpost on the right marks the track to Trwyn Cemlyn. The whole area can easily be enjoyed from this track and visitors should respect the reserve.

LLYN LLYWENAN   OS 106

This is the best inland water in Anglesey for wildfowl. Several species of duck breed in the surrounding reed beds, and in winter a large population often includes whooper swan.

WINTER: wigeon, teal, shoveler, pintail pochard, goldeneye, whooper swan, Canada goose.

SUMMER: tufted duck, shoveler, black-headed gull.

Leave the A5 on to the B5112, 1½ miles west of Gwalchmai. In 2 miles turn left at Trefor and take the third right after 2 miles. This unclassified road runs along the west and north sides of the lake and gives very good views.

NEWBOROUGH WARREN NATIONAL NATURE
RESERVE   OS 106; HT—0:53 Holyhead

The Reserve lies at the southern extremity of Anglesey, covers 1,566 acres, and is one of the best bird watching areas in Wales. The dune system of the Warren proper is the finest in Wales and is biologically very rewarding. A large area is now planted with conifers but open dunes and slacks, as well as part of the Cefri Estuary known as the Malltraeth Sands, are included in the Reserve. These sands are thronged by wildfowl and waders at all seasons. On passage the pool at the head of the estuary and separated from it by the sea wall, called The Cob, is excellent and regularly holds one of the best collections of waders in Wales. Unusual birds frequently appear.

WINTER: curlew, oystercatcher, wigeon, shelduck, pintail, peregrine.

SPRING: waders.

SUMMER: curlew, oystercatcher, herring gull.

AUTUMN: whimbrel, spotted redshank, godwits, little stint, sandpipers.

The whole area lies west of the A4080 and is reached from it. A track from the village of Newborough leads right through the reserve to the tip of the rugged Llanddwyn Island. At Malltraeth there is straightforward access at the sluices on to The Cob for good views over Malltraeth Sands and the Pool. The Cob even has cast iron seats for viewing the estuary. Apart from these and other rights of way marked on Reserve notice boards, permits are required for visitors and are obtainable from the Nature Conservancy, Penrhos Road, Bangor, but for ordinary bird-watching, the rights of way are quite adequate.

PUFFIN ISLAND   OS 106

Puffin Island lies less than a mile off Penmon Head to the south-eastern corner of Anglesey. It is under a mile long but exposes some quite large lengths of cliffs that provide breeding sites for a good variety of sea birds.

SUMMER: puffin, razorbill, guillemot, gulls, kittiwake, raven, shag, cormorant.

Cross the Menai bridge and turn right on to the A545 to Beaumaris where boats can be arranged.

SOUTH STACK, HOLYHEAD ISLAND   OS 106

This is the westernmost point of Anglesey and one of the best sea bird areas on the island. Though apparently ideally situated for sea-watching in autumn, there are no reports to date.

SUMMER: razorbill, guillemot, puffin, kittiwake.

AUTUMN: sea birds.

Leave Holyhead westwards on unclassified roads with OS map as guide.

Breconshire

BRECON BEACONS   OS 141

The Beacons lie to the south of Brecon and reach a maximum height of just under 3,000 feet. Though merely a desolate and

comparatively birdless moor in winter, summer brings a wealth
of species including the occasional merlin and peregrine. The
wooden valleys hold the typical species.

SUMMER: wheatear, buzzard, peregrine, merlin, red grouse,
ring ouzel, pied flycatcher, wood warbler, tree pipit, dipper,
nuthatch.

Hundreds of acres are 'open' but large areas belong to the
Forestry Commission and to various Municipal Water Boards.
It is accessible from the A470 near the Storey Arms, and from
the minor roads from Brecon, Tal-y-bont, and Pontsticill in the
south,

LLANGORSE LAKE   OS 141

The lake is situated at over 500 feet, 6 miles east of Brecon near
the Usk Valley. It is the largest natural lake in South Wales
and is surrounded by extensive reed-beds that give shelter
to waterfowl. Recent developments include motor boats, yachts,
canoes, and water-skiing, and many former residents are
being driven away.

The reed-beds hold a large fringe colony of reed warblers
which outnumber the sedge warblers. Yellow wagtails too
are on the edge of their range here. Migration is surprisingly
good and a large roost of sand martins gather in autumn.

WINTER: wild swans, pintail, goosander, Canada goose,
gulls.
SUMMER: great crested grebe, reed warbler, yellow wagtail.
AUTUMN: oystercatcher, greenshank, green sandpiper, dunlin,
ringed plover, commic and black terns.

Leave Brecon south-eastwards on the A40 and turn left on
to the B4560 at Bwlch. Continue to Llangorse village. Though
the land surrounding the lake is private, there are access points
at Llangorse village and Llangasty Church.

LLWYN-ON-RESERVOIR   OS 141

The reservoir lies 5 miles north of Merthyr Tydfil in the Taff
Valley and is surrounded by coniferous plantations. The summer population is augmented by passage waders in autumn,
and there are wildfowl in winter.

WINTER: wild swan, goldeneye.
SUMMER: buzzard, raven, dipper, heron, great crested grebe,
long-eared owl, common sandpiper.
AUTUMN: wood and green sandpipers, greenshank.

Leave Merthyr northwards on the A470 to the reservoir
on the left. There are public highways all round the lake.

TAL-Y-BONT RESERVOIR   OS 141
The water covers over 300 acres and lies at over 500 feet, 7 miles south-east of Brecon. It is the major haunt of wildfowl in the country. Cormorants are present in winter, and there is a small passage of waders in spring and autumn.

WINTER: wigeon, pochard, tufted duck, goldeneye, goosander, wild swans, cormorant.

SUMMER: common sandpiper, dipper, yellow wagtail, grasshopper warbler.

AUTUMN: greenshank, spotted redshank, oystercatcher, ruff.

Leave Brecon south-eastwards on the A40 but turn right after 2 miles on to the minor road running along the southern side of the Usk. Turn right at Tal-y-bont and view the reservoir from the road in 2 miles.

Caernarvonshire, Denbighshire and Flintshire

BARDSEY ISLAND BIRD OBSERVATORY
(Caernarvon)   OS 115
Bardsey is just under 2 miles south-west of the western tip of the Lleyn Peninsula. The island is $1\frac{3}{4}$ miles by three quarters of a mile and the main features are the 500 foot mountain in the east, the farmland area immediately west, and the southern lighthouse end joined to the main part by a narrow isthmus. The island has a varied breeding population and migrants are good on both passages, usually including a number of rarities. There is a resident warden.

SUMMER: chough, Manx shearwater, storm petrel.

SPRING AND AUTUMN: migrants, chats, warblers, flycatchers, melodious warbler.

Boats leave from Aberdaron and cost 10s. 0d. return. There is an island fee of 15s. 0d.

Accommodation must be booked in advance with Mrs. G. F. Walton, 51 Mount Road, St. Asaph, Flintshire. The charge is 11s. 0d. per night, including an evening meal, and full board at £8 8s. 0d. is available during some weeks in June and July.

CLWYD HILLS (Denbigh/Flint)   OS 108
These hills run between the Vale of Clwyd and the Dee Estuary. Though well below 2,000 feet the area is of significant ornithological interest and not to be by-passed on the way to Snowdonia.

SUMMER: merlin, red grouse, wheatear, ring ouzel, grasshopper warbler, whinchat, pied flycatcher, raven, buzzard.

The best area is around Moel Vammau and the best access is off the Ruthin–Mold summer road via Bwlch Pen Barras.

COLWYN BAY (Denbigh)   OS 107 and 108

Colwyn Bay stretches east of Rhos Point to Llanddulas. In spite of its heavily commercialised sea front, the area is a most important wintering ground for sea duck and a watch point for waders coasting westwards in autumn. Scoter (10,000) are dominant but velvet scoter are always present with up to 300 scaup.

WINTER: scoter, velvet scoter, merganser, scaup, wigeon, knot, turnstone, purple sandpiper, red-throated diver.

AUTUMN: waders.

The promenade at Colwyn stretches westwards all the way to Rhos Point, which is probably the best observation point. The coastal railway is crossed to the east at Llanddulas and Abergele, both good points for sea duck.

CONWAY ESTUARY (Caernarvon)
OS 107; HT −0:40 Liverpool

The estuary flows into the sea to the west of Great Ormes Head near Llandudno, and at Llandudno Junction is almost a mile wide. The commoner waders are numerous and reach a peak in autumn. This season also brings the rarer grebes most years.

WINTER: wigeon, teal, shelduck, pintail, oystercatcher, curlew.

SPRING: waders.

AUTUMN: whimbrel, greenshank, grebes.

The estuary can be worked from the eastern shore but only where there is access across the Conway Valley Railway. The three major vantage points are Glan Conway, Llandudno Junction, and Deganwy. A comprehensive view of the estuary may be had by taking the Llanrwst road (A496) a quarter of a mile east of Llandudno Junction. Proceed a quarter of a mile and park in the lay-by on the right of the road.

GREAT ORMES HEAD (Caernarvon)   OS 107

This is a tourist site of note and a very good cliff breeding sea bird colony. Though these species are the main attraction autumn brings an interesting passage of other sea birds.

SUMMER: guillemot, razorbill, puffin, kittiwake, fulmar, raven.

AUTUMN: Manx shearwater, gannet, scoter, terns.

Leave Llandudno northwards along the esplanade and continue along the coast road to the Head where there is a car park. Alternatively take the Great Orme Railway from Church Walks.

SHOTTON POOLS (Flint)   OS 109; HT +0:27 Liverpool

At the head of the Dee Estuary amongst a huge area of saltings and mud flats is a large steel works covering in all 1,000 acres. Amongst the buildings lie several natural freshwater pools and reed beds, and to the west are brackish lagoons, saltings and mud flats. In this uninspiring setting over 35 species regularly breed and a great many more visit. Dominating these visitors are large numbers of waders on both passages, though in August the reed beds provide a roost for up to 25,000 swallows. A high tide wader roost is best seen from the end of the ramp running westwards from the slag tip with 29 foot tides.

SPRING: waders.

SUMMER: shelduck, oystercatcher, common tern, reed warbler, wheatear, whinchat.

AUTUMN: greenshank, spotted redshank, ruff, green sandpiper, curlew sandpiper, little stint, swallow, sand martin.

Leave Chester westwards on the A548 and continue until it joins the A550. Turn left and enter works approach road, second on right, a quarter of a mile north of Queensferry Bridge.

The whole area is private land but permits are obtainable from The Works Relations Manager, John Summers and Sons Ltd, Hawarden Bridge Steelworks, Nr. Chester.

Do not venture into the tidal area when tides exceed 30 feet.

SNOWDONIA (Caernarvon)   OS 107

Snowdonia is contained within a rectangle joining Conway, Betws-y-Coed, Portmadoc and Caernarvon, yet to the climber and fell walker there is almost no need to look any further than the Llanberis pass and Ogwen Valley. It is a beautiful rugged landscape with bare grass and heather moors in the north, the peaks and mountain passes in the centre, and the beautiful wooded valleys to the south. Over such a vast area there are many good bird-watching places and the visitor is urged to make his own explorations.

The heather moor north of the Llyn-y-mynydd Reservoir west of Bethesda is worth a try for waders and grouse, and the Glaslyn valley south of Beddgelert is good for woodland species.

Choughs breed in some of the slate quarries, ring ouzels are found on the high screes, and a peregrine might be seen anywhere. Whooper swans are the only wildfowl of interest and almost the only inhabitants of the large lakes.

WINTER: whooper swan, buzzard, raven, peregrine, dipper.

SUMMER: buzzard, raven, dipper, grey wagtail, pied fly-catcher, chough, redstart, wood warbler, wheatear.

Walking over the area is generally permitted, though the usual courtesies are as important as anywhere. There are numerous paths which should be used wherever possible. The list of areas which follows is only intended as an outline guide:

1. Llyn Dinas, Lynan Mymbr, Cwm-y-Glo, often hold whooper swans.

2. The oak woods at Capel Curig, with their entrance across the bridged stream opposite the Corwen Hotel, are both beautiful and full of birds.

3. The A498 between Beddgelert and Prenteg is good for buzzards.

4. The moors north of Llyn-y-mynydd Reservoir and west of Bethesda for possible grouse, golden plover etc.

5. The first bridge north of Bethesda on the Nant Ffrancon for dipper and grey wagtail.

6. Cwm Idwal in the Ogwen Valley for wheatear, ring ouzel, beautiful scenery, and alpine flowers.

7. The woods around Betws-y-Coed for woodland species.

8. Vale of Ffestiniog for delicious and extensive oakwoods for pied flycatcher, etc.

There are several hotels to choose from at Llanberis, Capel Curig and Beddgelert, all are splendidly central. Climbers and walkers camp all over the place and there are many cheap 'barns' for those who rough it.

Cardiganshire and Carmarthenshire

CORS TREGARON (Cardigan)   OS 127 and 140

This area was declared a National Nature Reserve in 1955 and now extends to 1,898 acres. It is probably the finest example of a raised bog in England and Wales and is the only resort of Greenland white-fronts south of the Solway. Other wildfowl are regular in good numbers, as are hen harriers and other predators.

WINTER: white-fronted goose, wigeon, gadwall, pintail, shoveler, pochard, tufted duck, goldeneye, whooper swan, hen harrier.

SPRING: garganey.

SUMMER: buzzard, curlew, snipe.

Tregaron lies on the A485 between Lampeter and Aberystwyth, and the bog between the A485 and the B4343 along the River Teifi. Permits are required but a great deal can be seen from the roads and rights of way. Try the disused railway track across the northern half. The warden lives at Ty Coed, Nr. Tregaron and advises visitors.

DOVEY ESTUARY (Cardigan)

OS 127; HT –2:22 Holyhead

The estuary stretches inland for 5 miles and is nowhere less than a mile wide. The inter-tidal area is largely sand but with some extensive areas of mud and a good growth of salting, especially at the head of the estuary and around the Leri outfall near the mouth. The northern shore is bordered by hills with oak woods, while to the south there are extensive water meadows and nearer the mouth the peaty Borth Bog. The mouth is sheltered by the dune system of Twyni Bach. This variety of lowland makes the Dovey the most important centre for wildfowl in this part of Wales. Duck are numerous and Borth Bog, which is largely impassable, holds a flock of Russian white-fronts (maximum 500 in February–March). The usual sandy shore waders are present.

WINTER: wigeon, pintail, shelduck, merganser, white-fronted goose, redshank, oystercatcher, buzzard.
SPRING: waders.
SUMMER: warblers, pied flycatcher, redstart, buzzard.
AUTUMN: waders.

Using Aberdovey as a base, it is probably best to use the passenger ferry to Twyni Bach and cross Borth Bog on foot along the B4353 to see the geese.

Good views of the estuary proper can be obtained at many places from the A493 along the northern shore; and there are good views of the oak woods especially where that road turns north east at the head of the estuary, or around Tre'r-ddol in the south. There is a new reserve at Ynyshir, details from the RSPB.

GWENFFRWD (Cardigan)   OS 140

The RSPB has opened a reserve mainly for kites in the upper Towy valley 8 miles north of Llandovery. Details from the RSPB.

TAF, TOWY AND GWENDRAETH ESTUARIES
(Carmarthen)   OS 152; HT −0:11 Milford Haven

The three rivers share a communal mouth at the head of

Carmarthen Bay. There is an area of salting on the southern side of Gwendraeth, but the outstanding area of the Witchett Pool in the Laugharne Burrows is occupied by the military. There are fair sized flocks of the commoner dabbling duck, notably on the Taf, and sea duck are often numerous off Pendine. Waders are not outstanding but there is a good variety especially on passage. Turnstones occur at Salmon Point Scar, black-tailed godwit at Ferryside and both godwits on the Gwendraeth where there is the occasional wintering greenshank.

WINTER: wigeon, shoveler, pintail, godwits, grey plover, greenshank.

AUTUMN: golden plover, godwits, knot, turnstone.

The following are all good spots:

1. LAUGHARNE: leave the A40 southwards on the A4066 at St. Clears.

2. GINST POINT: leave the A4066 southwards via the Brill Road checkpoint when range not in use.

3. LLANSTEPHAN: leave the A40 1 mile west of Carmarthen southwards on the B4312.

4. FERRYSIDE: leave Carmarthen southwards on the A484 and turn right on unclassified roads after 6 miles to Ferryside.

5. GWENDRAETH AND SALMON POINT SCAR: leave the unclassified road between Ferryside and Kidwelly southwards on several tracks that pass under or over the railway. That at Tan-y-lan is good for both main areas.

Glamorganshire

EGLWYS NUNYDD RESERVOIR   OS 153

This is a recently filled reservoir covering 260 acres within the Steel Company of Wales' Margam site. It has part natural and part concrete banks and holds a good winter population of wildfowl, including several hundred diving duck. A small passage of waders is noted in spring and autumn and black terns are regular. A number of rarities have occurred in its short history, including spoonbill, purple heron and white-winged black tern.

WINTER: pochard, tufted duck, gadwall, goldeneye, scaup, smew, whooper and Bewick's swans, divers.

AUTUMN: sandpipers, spotted redshank, greenshank, black tern.

Leave the A48 on to the B4283 at Water Street, 4 miles east of Port Talbot. The reservoir is half a mile on the right through a private entrance. Permits are available from the Steel Company of Wales Ltd., Port Talbot, Glamorgan and are only issued to the following Societies: Ornithological Section Cardiff Naturalists' Society; Gower Ornithological Society; Glamorgan Naturalists' Trust; Monmouthshire Naturalists' Trust; local WAGBI associations; and the Nature Conservancy.

LAVERNOCK POINT   OS 154

The point lies at the south-east corner of the county on the Bristol channel 1 mile south of Penarth and consists of farmland with some scrub and open areas near the cliff tops. It is almost exclusively a migration spot with spring passage of a variety of species in small numbers from February to June. June and July see various sea birds offshore including Manx shearwater and gannet with occasional skuas and storm petrel, largely dependent on the weather. Autumn passage from July to November brings various warblers, a heavy and often dramatic hirundine and finch passage, and later the passage of winter thrushes. Rarities occur annually and have included kite, hobby, hoopoe, icterine and Bonelli's warblers, red-breasted flycatcher and ortolan bunting in recent years.

SPRING: visible migrants, chats and warblers.
SUMMER: Manx shearwater, gannet, raven.
AUTUMN: chats, warblers, flycatchers, hirundines, finches, thrushes, rarities.

Leave Penarth southwards on the B4267. Turn left half a mile past Lower Penarth and follow Fort Road to the coast. A coastal path leads from Penarth to the Point. The scrubland on cliff top is open to the public and this is the best spot.

OXWICH BAY   OS 153

The bay lies on the south side of the Gower Peninsula and consists of a 2 mile expanse of sand bounded by limestone cliffs and backed by sand-dunes, salt-marsh, fresh marshes and woodlands. An area of 542 acres is now a National Nature Reserve. Wildfowl are quite numerous and the small numbers of waders include sanderlings. Birds of prey are regularly noted. The variety of habitats enables a large range of species to find a niche including reed warblers that here reach their most westerly breeding haunt.

WINTER: wigeon, shoveler, sanderling.
SPRING AND AUTUMN: waders, warblers.
SUMMER: woodland and marsh species, sedge and reed warblers.

Leave the A4118 on the eastern road to Oxwich. This provides a transect of the various habitats and should be walked, many species can be seen from the road. Access to the east salt marsh is by a footpath on the left of the marsh road from the Oxwich Towers. Assistant Wardens are present in summer and a Nature Trail is laid out. Access to the fresh marsh is by permit (limited) from The Warden, The Small House, Llangennith, Nr. Swansea.

WHITEFORD BURROWS
OS 152; HT −0:08 Milford Haven

This is an extensive area of sand dunes and fir plantations on the north-western tip of the Gower peninsula at the mouth of the Burry Inlet. The Burrows belong to the National Trust and have been declared a National Nature Reserve. On the west side is the 2 mile stretch of Whiteford Sands and on the east Berges Island, the area of saltings around Landimore Marsh, and the Llanrhidian Sands. The wildfowl population is of great importance and includes large flocks of the commoner duck with small flocks of eider and brent geese. The odd diver is noted and both black-necked and Slavonian grebes are regular. Waders can be exceptionally numerous especially on passage and hen harriers and peregrines are present most winters.

WINTER: brent goose, wigeon, pintail, shelduck, divers, black-necked and Slavonian grebes, turnstone, bar-tailed godwit, knot, sanderling, oystercatcher, hen harrier, peregrine.

SPRING AND AUTUMN: bar-tailed godwit, turnstone, sanderling, grey plover, terns.

Leave Swansea westwards on the A4118. At the suburb of Killay turn right on to the B4396 and in 2½ miles join the B4295 to the left. Past Penclawdd this road runs along the shore and the area holds large flocks of shoveler. Continue to Llanrhidian and a maze of lanes to Cheriton. In a quarter of a mile this road merges with another on the left. Stop here. Take Frog Lane on the right hand side of the road. The track leads downhill above Burry Pill, past an old quarry, along the footpath to Pill House, across the sea wall, then turns north, skirting the sand dunes on the west. Continue along the path to the end of the Burrows, turn left for Whiteford Point, east for Berges Island.

WORMS HEAD
OS 152

A mile long rocky promontory at the south-western tip of the Gower peninsula near Rhossili, and is separated from the mainland at high tide. The Head is a National Nature Reserve and breeding birds include auks and gulls. Passage bring numbers

of shearwaters, terns and skuas offshore, and there are usually
large rafts of scoter in Rhossili Bay, and a few purple sandpipers on the Crabart in winter.

WINTER: scoter, purple sandpiper.

SPRING: Manx shearwater, terns.

SUMMER: guillemot, razorbill, greater black-backed and herring gulls, puffin.

AUTUMN: shearwaters, terns, skuas.

Leave the A4118 14 miles west of Swansea on to the B4247 to
Rhossili. A footpath leads along the cliff top to the Coastguard
Station which overlooks the head. The path continues down to
the rocky causeway which is uncovered for approximately 5½
hours, from 3½ hours after to 3¼ hours before high tide. Consult the tide tables at the Coastguard Station before crossing.
While crossing keep to northern side on approach, work across
to the middle of the causeway and veer again to the northern
side near Inner Head. Follow the easy footpath on the southern
side of Inner Head across the rocks at Low Neck and proceed
to Outer Head. There is no camping and birds and flowers
should not be disturbed.

Merionethshire and Montgomeryshire

DOVEY FOREST (Merioneth)   OS 116 and 127

The River Dulas has its source high in the forestry plantations
of the Dovey Forest. Throughout its short length it runs
through woodland forming an exceptionally beautiful valley.
The Dovey Forest is approximately 5 miles square and though
it consists largely of planted conifers there is a sprinkling of
natural or semi-natural oak and birch woods. There are certainly as many buzzards as anywhere in Britain and merlins can
be found on the tops.

SUMMER: buzzard, merlin, curlew, common sandpiper, dipper, grey wagtail, pied flycatcher, whinchat, redstart, wood
warbler, warblers, ring ouzel, redpoll.

There are two roads up the Dulas Valley, the A487 and an
unclassified road on the eastern side. This road continues upstream past Corris to Aberllefenni and beyond.

DULAS VALLEY (Montgomery)   OS 127

The Dulas runs south-east of Machynlleth and is a tributary of
the River Dovey. A number of smaller streams join the Dulas
from the south and east and together make an attractive and

rewarding area. Old oak woods and new plantations are quite extensive.

SUMMER: buzzard, pied flycatcher, redstart, tree pipit, ring ouzel, wheatear, whinchat.

Leave Machynlleth eastwards on the A489 and turn right up the Dulas Valley. Explore up to the tops by the mountain road to Bryn y Fedwen. Return and cross northwards into the Ffernant valley.

MAWDDACH ESTUARY (Merioneth)
OS 116; HT –2:15 Holyhead

The estuary stretches inland for some 5 miles to the Toll bridge at Penmaenpool. The seaside resort of Barmouth lies on the northern shore opposite the narrow outlet. The expanse of inter-tidal sand holds numbers of duck and occasional parties of whooper swans, as well as numbers of the commoner waders. The woodland along both banks, and especially the beautiful old oak woods, makes the area scenically outstanding.

WINTER: wigeon, teal, shelduck, whooper swan, oystercatcher, redshank, curlew, buzzard.

SUMMER: pied flycatcher, redstart, wood and other warblers, buzzard.

The A496 winds in and out among the woods and hills along the northern shore and gives excellent views at several spots across the estuary and to the sombre and impressive Cader Idris.

TRAETH BACH (Merioneth)
OS 116; HT −2:14 Holyhead

This is the largest part of the estuaries of the Glaslyn and the Dwyryd. The inter-tidal area stretches inland for 5 miles and though over 2 miles wide in parts, the mouth is little more than half a mile across because of the huge dune system of Morfa Harlech. The area supports a good population of waders of the commoner species in winter and a more varied population in autumn.

The wildfowl of the area are mainly found on the salt marsh of Glastraeth near Ynys Gifftan Island. The Glaslyn Pool, formed by the ballast bank at Portmadoc, is a regular haunt of whooper swans and the estuary mouth has a small flock of eider.

WINTER: wigeon, teal, shelduck, whooper swan, eider, oystercatcher, curlew, redshank.

SPRING AND AUTUMN: waders.

Glaslyn Pool and Traeth Mawr can be seen from the toll road (A497) along the ballast bank at Portmadoc.

Continue eastward on the A497 and in 1½ miles take the unclassified road across the Llandecwyn Railway Bridge. (Toll 1s. 0d. for a car.) Continue south on the A496 but turn right 1 mile past Talsarnau on to the B4573. Cross the river and turn sharp right where the road turns left. This metalled road leads to the shore.

Monmouthshire

CALDICOT LEVEL   OS 155

This area lies alongside the Severn to the west of the Severn Tunnel and consists of flat grazing land that is often flooded in winter and spring. Wild swans and a variety of duck are regular and quite large numbers of waders are often present.

WINTER AND SPRING: Bewick's and whooper swans, pintail, wigeon, shoveler, turnstone.

Leave the A48 between Newport and Chepstow southwards on the B4245 to Rogiet. Cross the railway at Severn Tunnel Junction and, keeping right, follow farm tracks towards Undy. The flooded area is on the right and can be inspected from a car.

There is access down lanes to the sea wall and coast for the Severn mudflats.

LLANDEGFEDD RESERVOIR   OS 155

Llandegfedd is a new reservoir covering some 400 acres, 3 miles south-east of Pontypool. Although its bird population has not settled down it has quickly become the most important inland water in the county. Large numbers of duck are noted together with great crested grebe. Passage is as yet little studied.

WINTER: wigeon, teal, pochard, tufted duck, coot.

SPRING AND AUTUMN: greenshank, knot, oystercatcher.

Leave Pontypool southwards on the A4042 and watch for signposts at New Inn. The reservoir lies to the left. Park at the dam and walk along the easterly shore. Access is by permit and these are held for members only by the Monmouth Ornithological Society and Monmouthshire Naturalists' Trust.

LLANTHONY VALLEY   OS 141 and 142

The valley lies 6 miles north of Abergavenny off the A465. The B4423 runs along this beautiful valley as far as Llanthony and a narrow lane continues into the heart of the Black Mountain

country to Hay. The beautiful Honddu stream runs between
steep hillsides and old oak woods. The typical upland birds are
found and the Sugar Loaf and Blorenge are worth climbing.

SUMMER: dipper, grey wagtail, pied flycatcher, buzzard, red
grouse, raven, ring ouzel.

Leave Abergavenny northwards on the A465 to Llanvihangel
Crucorney, turn left on the B4423 up the valley.

USK ESTUARY   OS 155; HT −0:11 Avonmouth
The Usk enters the sea south of Newport at the mouth of the
Severn. A large area of inter-tidal foreshore is exposed at low
tide providing feeding for wildfowl and waders. Though waders
are most plentiful in winter, passage should not be ignored.

WINTER: teal, wigeon, pochard, scaup, turnstone.

Leave Newport south-eastwards through Somerton to Gold-
cliff and view from the sea wall. Permission to walk along the
wall must be obtained at the farmhouse.

Pembrokeshire

GRASSHOLM   OS 138/151
The island of Grassholm lies 10 miles west of the mainland and,
covering 22 acres, is the smallest of the famous Pembrokeshire
islands. It is an RSPB reserve and is famous as the second largest
colony of gannets in Britain, numbering 15,500 pairs.

SUMMER: gannet, kittiwake, guillemot, razorbill.

Landing arrangements must be made with the West Wales
Naturalists' Trust, and landing is exceedingly difficult and in-
frequent. Nevertheless, Grassholm remains one of the most
accessible gannetries and well worth the effort.

GWAUN VALLEY   OS 138/151
The valley stretches south-east from Fishguard inland toward
the Presceli Mountains and is lined with old oak woods. The
usual upland species are found in beautiful surroundings and a
marshy flat valley bottom area near Sychbant is worth a look.

SUMMER: buzzard, redstart, wood warbler, dipper, grey wagtail.

Leave Fishguard south-eastwards on the B4313. Turn left
after 3 miles to Cilrhedyn and continue eastwards along the
valley.

MILFORD HAVEN   OS 138/151; HT at Milford Haven
The Haven is a huge tidal network stretching inland for 20

Milford Haven: showing the main access points grouped along the tributary valleys and bays

3 miles

⊛ = access

N

miles. The main bird-watching centres are on a series of shallow subsidiary channels at Gann mudflats, Angle Bay, Pembroke River, Cresswell River, Carew River and the two Cleddau Rivers. Wildfowl are present in some numbers, and the tiny Bicton Irrigation Reservoir regularly holds a number of duck and waders. Divers and grebes come into the Haven, especially during rough weather when they can be found at Dale Roads, Angle Bay and Pennar Gut. Waders of the normal estuarine species occur in winter and on passage but there are sometimes wintering black-tailed godwit, common sandpiper, and greenshank on the Gann.

WINTER: wigeon, pintail, shoveler, goldeneye, shelduck, divers, grebes, black-tailed godwit, common sandpiper, greenshank.

SPRING: whimbrel.

AUTUMN: whimbrel, turnstone, spotted redshank, ruff.

Access is at many good points:

1. RIVER GANN: can be seen from the B4327 north of Dale.
2. BICTON IRRIGATION RESERVOIR: can be seen from the road east of St. Ishmaels.
3. ANGLE BAY: view from the footpath that runs all the way way round, starting at Angle, B4320.
4. PEMBROKE RIVER: view from Lambeeth where a footpath leads east and west. Leave the B4320 northwards to Pwllcrocham and turn right at Wallaston Cross.
5. COSHESTON PILL: access from Waterloo on the north east side of Pembroke.
6. CAREW RIVER: access from West Williamson off A4075.
7. CRESSWELL RIVER: view from the road south of Lawrenny.
8. GARRON PILL: access at Garron north of Lawrenny.
9. LANDSHIPPING QUAY can be reached via a maze of lanes from Cross Hands on the A4075 where it joins A4115.
10. HOOK: leave Haverfordwest southwards on the A4076. Fork left at Merlin's Bridge and turn left in 3 miles. Walk along by river to Fowborough Point.

Accommodation is available for individuals and groups who wish to study birds in the area at Dale Fort and Orielton Field Centres under the auspices of the Field Studies Council. A number of courses on birds are organized every year and there are many opportunities for birding in the neighbourhood.

MINWEAR AND CANASTON WOODS
OS 138/151 and 152

These woods lie 7 miles east of Haverfordwest immediately

south of the A40. Minwear is mainly deciduous and Canaston consists of conifers of varying ages. The Forestry Commission have opened a marked trail.

SUMMER: wood warbler, redstart, nightjar, tree pipit.

Leave the A40 southwards on the A4075. The first on the right leads to Minwear, on the left to Canaston.

RAMSEY ISLAND   OS 138/151

The island lies half a mile off the northern arm of St. Bride's Bay, covers 650 acres, and is a RSPB reserve with a resident warden. It is an attractive island with cliffs rising to 170 feet on which choughs breed.

SUMMER: chough, razorbill, guillemot, kittiwake, fulmar, stonechat, wheatear, buzzard.

Permits, 5s. 0d., and 2s. 6d. for children, are obtainable on landing, or from the official boatman, but this does not include the cost of transport. Boats leave from the lifeboat station at St. Justinian's, 1½ miles west of St. David's, where the name of the boatman and times of departure are displayed. A furnished bungalow is available, cost 7s. 6d. per head per night.

ST. ANN'S HEAD   OS 138/151

St. Ann's Head lies at the entrance to Milford Haven and is remarkably convenient to Dale and Dale Fort Field Centre, should visitors to Skokholm have to wait for the swell to subside. Gannets and Manx shearwaters are frequently noted just offshore and there are interesting breeding species.

WINTER: divers, grebes.

SUMMER: chough, fulmar, shag, gannet, Manx shearwater.

Leave Dale, at the end of the B4327, southward to the Head – only one road. See Map, page 139.

SKOKHOLM BIRD OBSERVATORY   OS 138/151

Skokholm lies 2 miles west of the mainland, the same distance south of Skomer, and is 1 mile by half a mile. Emphasis on the island is on migration and the work is organized by the Field Studies Council in conjunction with the Edward Grey Institute, Oxford. Sea bird movements are interesting and migration of chats, warblers, and flycatchers is often heavy. The October migration of finches and thrushes is sometimes dramatic and this month is usually very good for rarities, such as redbreasted flycatcher, yellow-browed warbler, and Lapland bunting. Breeding birds include storm petrel and well studied Manx shearwater.

SPRING: migrant passerines.

SUMMER: Manx shearwater, guillemot, razorbill, storm petrel.
AUTUMN: shearwaters, gannet, kittiwake, skuas, waders,
thrushes, finches, chats, warblers, flycatchers, rarities.
Accommodation is available at £9 10s. per week, full board.
Access is on Saturdays and the boat from Dale costs 10s. 0d.
return. Arrangements are made to meet the night train from
Paddington at Haverfordwest and transport visitors to Dale
Fort for breakfast – transport 10s. 0d. return. All visitors must
become members of the West Wales Naturalists' Trust which
costs 10s. 6d. Usual conditions concerning delays and weather.
Enquiries to The Warden, Dale Fort Field Centre, Haverford-
west, Pembrokeshire.

SKOMER ISLAND   OS 138/151
The island lies 1 mile off the coast and is the largest, most accessible and in many ways the best of the four Pembrokeshire
islands. Covering 752 acres, its towering cliffs surround a flat
plateau at about 200 feet. It is composed of grey, igneous rocks
like Grassholm but unlike Skokholm, which is old red sandstone. The island was declared a National Nature Reserve in
1959 and is administered by the West Wales Naturalists' Trust,
who appoint a warden. Manx shearwaters and puffins are the
most abundant birds but others include storm petrel and
chough.
    Migrants are exciting and include sea birds, passerine falls
and rarities but are not intensively studied as they are at Skokholm.
SUMMER: Manx shearwater, storm petrel, fulmar, puffin,
razorbill, guillemot, kittiwake, stonechat, chough, buzzard,
short-eared owl, peregrine.
A guide and trail is laid out for visitors and the island is
open daily during the summer. Visitors who are not members
of the West Wales Naturalists' Trust pay 5s. 0d. landing fee
(2s. 6d. for children). Normally a boat runs from Martins Haven
leaving at 10.30 a.m. Intending visitors should contact the
WWNT before departure, especially outside the main season,
though weather permitting the boat leaves daily Whitsun–
August. Limited accommodation is available to West Wales
Naturalists' Trust members at 5s. 0d. per night on a hostel
basis, enquiries to the Trust Secretary.

STACK ROCKS, FLIMSTON   OS 138/151
These rocks are limestone cliffs and stacks 6 miles south-west
of Pembroke, and hold good colonies of sea birds.

SUMMER: chough, guillemot, razorbill, kittiwake, fulmar, herring gull.

Leave Pembroke southwards on the B4319 and turn left after 7 miles to Flimston. Access to the coast is allowed across the tank range when the red flag is not flying. Also good cliff walk to St. Govan's Head.

Part 3: Scotland

Aberdeenshire, Banffshire, Kincardineshire, Morayshire and Nairnshire

CULBIN BAR AND FOREST (Nairn/Moray)
                              OS 29; HT −0:05 Inverness
This area lies on the Nairn-Moray border 3 miles east of the town of Nairn. A 5 mile long sand bar has been built up offshore and areas of salting flank either side of the channel between the bar and the mainland. Culbin Forest covers most of the land away from the shore and is 6 miles by 1½ miles. At its western end are Loch Loy and Cran Loch, two large freshwater pools among the pines.

The bar holds a variety of breeding birds, including all the British terns except roseate. The pine forest has an excellent collection of species that bird-watchers flock to see at Speyside. Crossbill, crested tit, capercaillie and siskin all breed, as do nightjars in some of the more open spaces. The wildfowl of the area are centred on the channel and include large numbers of sea duck, while the forest lochs hold fresh species and whooper swans.

WINTER: wigeon, scoter, velvet scoter, merganser, pintail, tufted duck, goldeneye, whooper swan, redshank, curlew, dunlin.

SPRING: waders, crossbill.

SUMMER: eider, shelduck, merganser, common, Arctic, Sandwich and little terns, crossbill, crested tit, capercaillie, siskin, goldcrest, nightjar.

AUTUMN: waders, gannet, Arctic skua.

Leave Forres westwards on A96 and immediately after crossing the Findhorn River, fork right on minor roads to Kintessack village. To take a car into the forest apply to Mr. Milne, the head forester. Otherwise continue through the village to Welhill gate and park, continuing on foot. The bar is accessible at most states of the tide if the county boundary is followed exactly. *No smoking* in the forest – *absolutely essential*.

FOWLSHEUGH CLIFFS (Kincardine)   OS 43
The cliffs stand 3 miles south of Stonehaven, immediately north of Henry's Scorth which is marked on the OS map. Though not high, they are one of the most important sea bird

stations on this coast, and their rubbly and indented nature make for easy viewing.

SUMMER: razorbill, guillemot, kittiwake, fulmar.

Leave Stonehaven southwards on the A92 and turn left after 3½ miles to Crawton. Walk northwards on cliff footpath for threequarters of a mile.

PENNAN HEAD (Banff) OS 31

Situated 9 miles west of Fraserburgh and half a mile east of the small coastal village of Pennan. The main attraction is the breeding sea birds on the 350 foot high cliffs. Peregrines are often seen and house martins nest on the cliffs and in caves.

SUMMER: guillemot, razorbill, puffin, kittiwake, fulmar, peregrine, house martin.

Leave Fraserburgh on the A98 and turn right on to the B9032 at Ardlaw. After 1½ miles continue on the B9031 and after a further 7½ miles turn right to Pennan. Access along cliff tops eastward to the Head. The cliffs are dangerous.

SPEY MOUTH (Moray)

OS 29 and 30; HT −0:12 Inverness

For its final 4 miles, the Spey is a network of channels and islands with areas of alder swamp. As it enters the sea there is a sand bar and a considerable inter-tidal area. The bar and offshore area holds numbers of sea duck in spring. Terns breed on the shingle islands with a wealth of small birds, and autumn passage brings waders and sea birds offshore.

WINTER: wigeon, teal, turnstone, bar-tailed godwit, cormorant.

SPRING: goldeneye, long-tailed duck, merganser.

SUMMER: common and Arctic terns, stonechat, corn bunting.

AUTUMN: whimbrel, greenshank, merganser, velvet and common scoter, red-throated diver, gannet.

Access is simple from Spey Bay village on the east side. On the western and more interesting side, access is from Garmouth and Kingston via the B9015 from Mosstodloch, 1½ miles west of Fochabers. At Garmouth cross the golf course past the club house to reach the river. Viewing from Kingston is excellent.

LOCH OF STRATHBEG (Aberdeen) OS 31

The loch lies at the easternmost corner of Scotland near Rattray Head between Fraserburgh and Peterhead. A storm in 1715 closed the Crimond Burn and formed this 500 acre loch, 2 miles by half a mile. It is separated from the sea by less than half a mile of sand and shingle and is surrounded by marshy vegetation and reeds. All of these factors combine to make the

Loch of Strathbeg one of the most attractive and exciting places to watch birds in Scotland.

The winter population of wildfowl is varied and includes up to 8,000 mallard, the largest flock in Britain (see Rostherne Mere, Cheshire). Greylags and pinkfeet number up to 2,000 in autumn with the latter reaching 5,000 in spring. Up to 600 whooper swans have been noted in autumn and a pond at near-by Pittenheath has the only regular Bewick's swans in Scotland.

In summer a wide variety of species breed, and eider and great crested grebe can be seen together. Passage brings terns and waders.

WINTER: mallard, wigeon, pochard, tufted duck, goldeneye, goosander, greylag and pink-footed geese, whooper swan.

SPRING: pink-footed goose.

SUMMER: terns, eider, great crested grebe.

AUTUMN: marsh harrier, greylag and pink-footed geese, whooper and mute swans, terns, green sandpiper.

Leave the A952 between Fraserburgh and Peterhead east-wards on unclassified roads 1 mile south of Crimond. Views of the loch can be obtained northwards near the old chapel and there is general access along the dunes.

TROUP HEAD (Banff)   OS 31

Troup Head is 10 miles east of Banff and forms 350 feet high cliffs that are the haunt of large numbers of sea birds. House martins breed in caves at the extreme eastern end of the area. The long sea tunnel known as Hell's Lum with its enormous blow holes some distance inland is a non-ornithological must.

SUMMER: guillemot, razorbill, puffin, kittiwake, fulmar, house martin.

Leave Banff eastwards on the A98 and turn left after 2 miles on to the B9031. 1¾ miles past the Gardenstown signpost turn left to Northfield Farm and park. Walk northwards to the head of a large gully and follow its left bank to the headland.

YTHAN ESTUARY (Aberdeen)
OS 40; HT +2:07 Aberdeen

Situated 13 miles north of Aberdeen between Newburgh and Ellon. Though 3 miles long the estuary is nowhere much more than quarter of a mile wide and birds can be seen at close range. The 1,774 acre expanse of the Sands of Forvie borders the northern side of the estuary for its lower half and was made a National Nature Reserve in 1959. Sand dunes also border the estuary on the southern shore and both areas hold breeding colonies of terns, gulls and eider.

Little Loch

Meikle Loch

B9003

Cotehill Loch

Sand Loch

Collieston

A975

waders gather here at H.T.

Sands of Forvie National Nature Reserve

Tarty Burn

River Ythan

N

Newburgh

B9000

1 mile

Foveran Links

Ythan Estuary: the A975 provides ideal vantage points to north and south of the bridge, and the lochs to the north of the Sands of Forvie are not to be missed

Upstream mud flats and mussel beds are frequented by eider and flocks of wintering waders and wildfowl, including about 1,000 each of greylag and pinkfeet. The lochs to the north, including Cotehill and Sand inside the Reserve, and Meikle, three-quarters of a mile to the north, hold duck. Autumn brings hordes of waders and Arctic skuas frequently come up stream to chase the numerous terns.

WINTER: greylag and pink-footed geese, wigeon, scaup, goldeneye, long-tailed duck, tufted duck, pochard, goosander, eider, common and velvet scoter, divers, knot, golden plover, redshank, snow bunting.

SPRING: terns, waders, eider.

SUMMER: eider, shelduck, common, Arctic, Sandwich and little terns, black-headed gull, ringed plover, red grouse, stonechat.

AUTUMN: terns, skuas, grey plover, turnstone, bar-tailed and black-tailed godwits, whimbrel, green sandpiper, spotted redshank, curlew sandpiper, ruff, warblers, chats, flycatchers.

Leave Aberdeen northwards on the A92 and fork right after 12 miles on to the A975 to Newburgh. The road then runs alongside the estuary, crosses it, and continues along the eastern bank. At high tide waders congregate around the Tarty Burn, which can be approached along the estuary on the west side.

The Reserve is approached via Collieston on the B9003, though Cotehill and Meikle Lochs can be seen from roads and tracks. Authority to enter the Reserve must be obtained during the summer and autumn from the Nature Conservancy Scottish Office.

Angus, Clackmannanshire, Fifeshire, Kinross-shire and Perthshire

EDEN ESTUARY (Fife)

OS 56; HT +1:00 Aberdeen

The estuary of the Eden is 2 miles north of St. Andrews with the famous golf links on the sand bar at its mouth. It is 3 miles long and for most of its length under 1 mile wide. The expanse of mud is frequented by vast numbers of wildfowl and waders in winter. The area at the mouth holds huge rafts of scoter almost throughout the year. Eiders too are numerous, and both species come inshore to shelter on the east side of Shelly Point in rough weather. This shingle spit is the main wader roost and holds colonies of breeding terns. It is, however, unprotected and is becoming a bathing beach and doubtless the terneries will now decline. The bay between the point and the mainland is a haunt of passage waders and little gulls are noted in spring.

WINTER: wigeon, teal, pintail, shoveler, goldeneye, scoter, eider, knot, oystercatcher, godwits, curlew.

SPRING: black-tailed godwit, grey plover, little gull.

SUMMER: common, Arctic, Sandwich and little terns.

AUTUMN: black-tailed and bar-tailed godwits, grey plover, whimbrel, spotted redshank, ruff, terns.

Leave St. Andrews northwards along the coast on the seaward side of the golf links to Out Head which is half a mile from Shelly Point. Views can also be obtained from Cable Shore, 3 miles north-west of St. Andrews, and from the outer bridge across the Mottray Water at Guard Bridge.

FLANDERS MOSS AND LAKE OF MENTEITH
(Perth)   OS 54

The area lies south-east of Aberfoyle between the arms of the A81. Flanders Moss is a great peat bog, in many places impassable, that shelters a variety of breeding and wintering birds. The Lake of Menteith is 1½ miles long and is known as a haunt of wildfowl. Recent disturbance by water-skiing has reduced its attractiveness and geese are now more often found on the Moss and on Loch Rusky.

WINTER: greylag and pink-footed geese, goldeneye, whooper swan, great grey shrike, hen harrier.

SPRING: greylag and bean geese.

SUMMER: black-headed and lesser black-backed gulls, woodcock, heron, golden plover, curlew, goosander, red and black grouse, raven.

AUTUMN: pink-footed goose, hen harrier.

Leave Aberfoyle southwards on the A821, at its junction with the A81.

1. Turn right and stop in 1 mile at the bridge over the railway and the River Forth. Walk eastwards along the old railway track to the river and follow bank out on to West Moss. This land is private and permission should be sought locally.

2. Turn left and view Lake of Menteith in 2¼ miles. Continue and turn right in a further mile on to the B8034 for further views.

3. Turn left and leave the A81 southwards at Thornhill on the B822. At the bend in the road walk westwards for 2½ miles on to East Moss.

Anywhere on the moss is heavy and wet going, gumboots are essential.

FORFAR LOCHS (Angus)   OS 50
Immediately west of the town is the Loch of Forfar, while 3 miles to the east are Rescobie and Balgavies Lochs. All are good for wildfowl, can be seen from the road, and are thus

ideal for the casual visitor. Geese are generally absent but mute and whooper swans are regular with a wide variety of duck.

WINTER: wigeon, shoveler, pochard, tufted duck, goldeneye, goosander, mute and whooper swans.

LOCH OF FORFAR: leave Forfar westwards on unclassified roads.

RESCOBIE LOCH: leave Forfar eastwards on the B9133 view to the south after 3 miles.

BALGAVIES LOCH: As for Rescobie but continue eastwards and turn right. In threequarters of a mile view westwards and turn right at the A932 and view to the north.

LARGO BAY, KILCONQUHAR LOCH AND ELIE
NESS (Fife)   OS 56; HT −0:10 Leith

These three spots lie in a compact area on the northern shore of the Forth east of Leven. Though waders occur at all seasons the area is mainly noted for wildfowl and sea birds. Largo Bay holds several hundred scoter in winter, and there is a notable double passage of up to 200 long-tailed duck. Kilconquhar Loch covers 100 acres and is nowhere deeper than 6 feet. Its winter population includes numbers of duck and 300 greylag geese. Both the loch and Largo Bay are haunts of little gulls in autumn. Lundin Links is the most reliable but the loch has held over 500 of these birds. Elie Ness usually has a few in autumn and this is the best place to watch for divers, auks, terns, skuas and shearwaters on both passages.

WINTER: scoter, tufted duck, pochard, goldeneye, shoveler, wigeon, greylag goose.

SPRING: long-tailed duck, waders, divers, terns.

SUMMER: pochard, grasshopper warbler.

AUTUMN: little gull, black tern, divers, waders, auks, terns, roseate tern, skuas, shearwaters, long-tailed duck.

LUNDIN LINKS: leave the A915 half a mile west of Lower Largo southwards to the station. Turn right and pass under the railway.

LARGO BAY: leave Lower Largo eastwards along the front and continue on foot around the Bay.

ELIE NESS: directly accessible on the eastern side of Elie.

KILCONQUHAR LOCH: visible from roads on north side and from churchyard.

SHELL BAY: leave the A917 westwards near Kilconquhar Loch on minor road and track. Ruddons Point is accessible when firing is not taking place on nearby ranges.

LOCH LEVEN (Kinross)   OS 55

Loch Leven lies midway between the Firths of Forth and Tay immediately east of Kinross. The National Nature Reserve covers 3,946 acres and is the most important inland water in Britain for wildfowl. It is the main arrival area for pinkfeet which number 12,000 in autumn, and several hundred greylags and a few bean also use the loch as a staging post. Pinkfeet decline to a winter level of 1,000 but build up again in spring, when greylags sometimes number 3,000. Wigeon, teal, pochard and tufted have all topped 1,000 and breeding duck are important.

A great variety of other species occur including waders, terns and gulls. Whooper swans number 400 in autumn.

WINTER: greylag and pink-footed geese, wigeon, pochard, tufted duck, shoveler, goldeneye, goosander, whooper swan.

SPRING: greylag and pink-footed geese, waders.

SUMMER: tufted duck, shoveler, gadwall, mute swan.

AUTUMN: greylag, pink-footed and bean geese, mute swan, waders, terns. Access to the reserve is confined to:

1. KIRKGATE PARK, Kinross.

2. BURLEIGH SANDS, 2 miles north-east of Kinross on the A911.

3. FINDATIE, in the south-eastern corner of the Loch off the B9097.

4. LOCH LEVEN CASTLE.

5. VANE FARM, a RSBP reserve in the south-eastern corner of the loch on the B9097 will be open from 1 October, 1967.

ISLE OF MAY (Fife)   OS 56

The island stands at the mouth of the Firth of Forth, 5 miles south-east of Anstruther and covers 140 acres. Though known since 1907 as a migration watch point, this attractive island holds a good population of breeding sea birds on the cliffs.

Migrants include large numbers of thrushes, pipits, goldcrests and finches in early spring and late autumn. The commoner warblers, chats and flycatchers occur in largest numbers in autumn when most rarities turn up. These have included barred warbler, bluethroat, ortolan bunting and vagrants like Raddes' bush warbler, yellow-breasted bunting, etc. Waders are usually quite numerous and the passage of shearwater sometimes includes sooty.

SPRING: thrushes, finches, goldcrest, warblers, chats.

SUMMER: razorbill, guillemot, puffin, kittiwake, fulmar, shag, gulls, rock pipit, wheatear.

AUTUMN: turnstone, whimbrel, purple sandpiper, little stint, spotted redshank, Manx and sooty shearwaters, Arctic and great skuas, warblers, chats, flycatchers, barred warbler, bluethroat, ortolan, snow and Lapland buntings, thrushes, finches, rarities.

The island is reached by boat from Anstruther, 15s. 0d. return.

Accommodation is available on hostel lines at 5s. 0d. per night. Enquiries to Miss N. J. Gordon, 12 Hope Terrace, Edinburgh 9.

MORTON LOCHS (Fife)   OS 56
The lochs, 1 mile south of Tayport, are a National Nature Reserve covering 59 acres. They lie in the area that includes Tentsmuir Point also a National Nature Reserve, Earlshall Moor and Shelly Point which is dealt with under the Eden Estuary. The lochs are known as a wintering and breeding haunt of many duck. In spring and autumn waders, including 'fresh' species, are abundant, if the water level is low. Nearly 130 species have been recorded, including 45 breeding.

WINTER: wigeon, teal, shoveler, tufted duck, whooper swan.
SPRING: waders, little gull.
SUMMER: shoveler, tufted duck, gadwall, waders, stonechat, sedge warbler, corn bunting.
AUTUMN: godwits, green sandpiper, spotted redshank, little stint, curlew sandpiper, ruff.

Leave Tayport southwards on the B945 and turn left after 2 miles on to the track that separates the lochs. Though a great deal can be seen from this road, permits enabling one to use the hides on either side of the northern loch can be obtained from the Nature Conservancy Scottish Office.

FIRTH OF TAY (Fife)
                    OS 50, 55, and 56; HT +1:30 Aberdeen
The Firth cuts deep into the Scottish coast and from Budden Ness to Perth is nearly 30 miles of tidal water and some of the most outstanding bird haunts in Scotland. For our purpose the whole area is divided into three parts:

1. The Flats at the mouth west of Tentsmuir.
2. The Buddon Burn area on the north shore.
3. The estuary above Dundee along the northern bank.

1. *Tentsmuir* (OS 50 and 56) lies at the mouth of Tay on the southern shore with extensive flats to the west. Flocks of sea duck occur immediately offshore including a large gathering of long-tailed duck in early spring. Waders are numerous and snow buntings are often abundant in autumn.

WINTER: eider, scoter, scaup, wigeon, merganser, pink-footed goose, knot, bar-tailed godwit, snow bunting.

SPRING: long-tailed duck, little gull.

SUMMER: eider, scoter.

AUTUMN: bar-tailed godwit, whimbrel, greenshank, curlew sandpiper, little stint.

Leave Tayport southwards and turn left after 2 miles past Morton Lochs to Morton and on to Fetterdale. A maze of forest drives leads to the point. No access for vehicles within the reserve.

2. *Buddon Burn* (OS 50; HT +1:20 Aberdeen) lies on the northern shore at the mouth of the Tay 1 mile east of Monifieth. The small stream enters the sea through a tiny bay amongst the dunes at the western end of Buddon. The fresh water attracts a number of species but is outstanding as a haunt of little gulls particularly in spring, but the species is present throughout the summer and autumn. Over 50 have been recorded.

SPRING: little gull, sanderling.

SUMMER: little tern.

AUTUMN: little gull.

Walk eastwards along the shore from Monifieth.

3. *Tay Estuary* (OS 55 and 56), west of Dundee the Estuary is up to 3 miles wide with extensive mud banks along the northern shore. Above Powgavie the shore is fringed by large reed beds that shelter a variety of breeding birds. The mud banks are an important roost for pink-feet, up to 20,000 appearing in autumn and 5,000 remaining for the winter. Greylags (up to 2,000) also occur but prefer the area around Mugdrum Island. Goldeneye are especially numerous off Newburgh in spring and vast assemblages of waders occur on passage and in winter.

WINTER: pink-footed and greylag geese, tufted duck, goosander, merganser, goldeneye, knot, dunlin, bar-tailed godwit.

SPRING: goldeneye, waders.

AUTUMN: knot, godwits, grey plover, whimbrel, little stint.

There are several access points, as follows:

1. KINGOODIE: leave Dundee westwards on the A85 and turn left on to the B958 at Invergowrie.

2. POWGAVIE: continue on the B958 to Powgavie and take the road straight to the shore.

3. PORT ALLEN: continue on the B958 and turn left.

4. NEWBURGH: take the ferry from Dundee to Newport and turn westwards on the A914. At its junction with the A913 turn right to Newburgh and view Mugdrum Island.

Argyllshire, Inverness-shire and Inner Hebrides

CAIRNGORMS (Inverness)   OS Tourist Map Cairngorms
The mountains between the Spey and its tributary the Feshie River, and the Dee and its tributary the Geldie Burn. The area forms a geographical unity some 10 miles square which constitutes one of the largest nature reserves in Europe. The main peaks are all about 4,200 feet mark and the high plateau forms the most extensive 'alpine-arctic' habitat in Britain. Ptarmigan, dotterel and snow bunting are found in that order of abundance, but it is possible to tramp over all the tops for a day and still not see a sign of any of these birds. Further west the country becomes more rugged and golden eagle, buzzard, peregrine and merlin become more numerous along with greenshank and red grouse.
   WINTER: snow bunting.
   SUMMER: ptarmigan, dotterel, snow bunting, golden eagle, peregrine, merlin, greenshank.
   Restrictions on access are confined to parts of Mar and Glenfeshie in August-October, otherwise the visitor is free to walk the 58,000 acres as he will.
   The opening up of the Cairngorms as a tourist area has made the high tops easily accessible to all via the chair-lift at the head of Glen More.
   No matter how strong and energetic the bird-watcher the Cairngorms are no place for the beginner. Day walkers should carry one inch OS map, preferably cloth, compass and be suitably equipped with food and clothing.
   Speyside has a range of accommodation, but try Braemar which is also convenient for the Forests of Mar and Derry with crested tit, etc.

ISLAY (Argyll)   OS 57
Islay is one of the most beautiful and varied of Scottish islands. It measures 26 miles from north to south and is large enough for a long holiday of exploration. Its varied habitats include woodland, moors, cliffs, dunes, machair, lochs and sea lochs. Winter is probably the best season, for by February Islay holds 10,000 barnacle geese or one sixth of the world's population. Greenland white-fronts reach 3,000 about the same time, and 500 greylags winter. Most of these geese can be seen on the huge shallow sea loch, Loch Indaal, but the biggest flocks are

on the north-western part of the island. Loch Indaal also holds most of the sea duck that winter, great northern divers are numerous, and whooper swans and glaucous gulls regular.

Over 100 species breed, including the occasional scoter; black guillemot at Port Askaig for instance; golden eagle and outstandingly one of Scotland's two colonies of chough on Oa (the other is on nearby Jura). Perhaps the Arctic skua breeds.

WINTER: barnacle, white-fronted and greylag geese, scaup, eider, merganser, wigeon, shelduck, whooper swan, glaucous gull, great northern diver.

SPRING: great northern diver, whimbrel, turnstone.

SUMMER: merganser, eider, auks, black guillemot, kittiwake, terns, golden eagle, buzzard, chough.

AUTUMN: Manx shearwater, skuas, black-tailed godwit, greenshank, sanderling, curlew sandpiper, little stint.

MacBraynes run a daily (except Sunday) service between Gourock/Tarbert/Islay which is on two steamers and a short bus ride. This is increased to twice daily two days each week during July-August.

Between West Loch Tarbert and Gigha in winter the sea holds velvet scoter, long-tailed duck, Slavonian grebe, and huge numbers of great northern divers. The return fare is 56s. 7d. excluding the bus, and cars can be carried on all sailings from Tarbert.

BEA run a daily service from Glasgow (Renfrew) and by air Islay is 4½ hours from London. Choughs are frequently seen at the airport.

There is plenty of accommodation and cars can be hired. Write to Islay, Jura and Colonsay Tourist Association, District Offices, Bowmore.

RHUM (Inverness)   OS 33
This was for long a forbidden island but since 1957 has been a National Nature Reserve covering 26,400 acres, or about 8 miles square. It rises to 2,659 feet and is one of the wettest places in Britain, lying 15 miles west of Mallaig and immediately south-west of Skye. The island is grass covered, with patches of heather, mountain lichens and mosses, and some areas of trees around Loch Scresort and Papadil Lodge. It is now used as an outdoor laboratory and research includes an intensive study of the population of red deer.

Birds include an interesting colony of several thousand pairs of Manx shearwaters, near the top of Askival, at a height of 2,500 feet as well as cliff breeding sea birds. Two or three pairs of golden eagles and peregrines breed annually.

SUMMER: Manx shearwater, guillemot, razorbill, puffin, fulmar, black guillemot, kittiwake, eider, golden eagle, peregrine, golden plover, merlin, red-throated diver, merganser, corncrake, rock dove, common gull, Arctic tern, goldcrest, twite.

Day visitors are free to land at Loch Scresort and explore the area on the south side of the loch. Permission to go beyond this must be sought from the Wardens at White House, Kinloch or Bayview Kinloch. Bird-watchers, and other naturalists, wishing to study any particular feature of the island's natural history should write to the Nature Conservancy Scottish Office as far in advance as possible. Every effort will be made to provide facilities for research, but there is no accommodation. Only scientists, naturalists and climbers can stay on Rhum.

MacBraynes' steamers leave Mallaig three times a week for Rhum. The crossing takes 3–3½ hours and costs 19s. 6d. return. The Saturday departure leaves at 6 a.m. and allows 9 hours ashore, but arrangements may be changed annually.

SPEYSIDE AT ABERNETHY FOREST AND LOCH GARTEN (Inverness)   OS Tourist Map Cairngorms

The forest and loch lie on the eastern side of the Spey valley 8 miles downstream from the more renowned Rothiemurchus, near Nethybridge and Boat of Garten. Bird watchers have for too long concentrated on Rothiemurchus, and Abernethy has been consequently neglected though it is almost as rich in birds.

Basically the area is much the same as Rothiemurchus with scattered growth of old Scots pines and new plantations, with birches and juniper bushes, and heather and small berry plants. The small passerines include the specialities, crested tit, crossbill and siskin, but Abernethy has the ospreys at Loch Garten as a unique attraction. Capercaillies are numerous and the only large-scale display ground of this species in the country is in Abernethy.

In spring many northern species stay very late, displaying and look as if they are settling down to breed. Goldeneye, redwing, brambling are all regular in May.

WINTER: whooper swan, goldeneye, hen harrier, short-eared owl, crossbill.

SPRING: redwing, goldeneye, brambling, crossbill.

SUMMER: crested tit, siskin, grouse, capercaillie, long-eared owl, golden eagle, peregrine, merlin, greenshank, woodcock.

Leave the A95 eastwards to either Nethybridge or Boat of Garten on the B970. A ring road runs from both up to Loch Garten which is 'osprey sign-posted' in summer. This road makes an excellent basis for exploration which is facilitated by a series of forest tracks heading up into the mountains east of Abernethy proper. Excellent views of breeding ospreys can be obtained from the RSPB hides near the Loch Garten eyrie.

SPEYSIDE AT ROTHIEMURCHUS AND GLEN MORE (Inverness)

OS Tourist Map Cairngorms

This is one of the outstanding bird haunts in Britain. The area stretches from Aviemore in the north to Insh, 9 miles south and up to the Cairngorms east of Loch Morlich. The Forest of Abernethy, including Loch Garten, and the Cairngorms, are treated separately. The whole can be divided into several quite distinct parts, all of which should be visited. The Spey valley itself and the large Loch Insh with its marshy inlet are the haunt of wildfowl in winter. To the west lie the birch woods of Craigellachie (250 acres) which have been incorporated into a National Nature Reserve and which abound with birds, indeed Rothiemurchus seems deserted in comparison. From the top of Craigellachie the huge basin of Rothiemurchus lies before one, mingling in to the Glen More Forest further north with Meall a' Bhuachaille separating the whole from Abernethy, and the Cairngorms massively enclosing the area from the east. This basin is the chief haunt of the crested tit and Scottish crossbill and holds many other interesting species. The area also lies on the line separating carrion from hooded crow and though neither is numerous, both forms breed.

SPRING: goldeneye, whooper swan, golden eagle, crossbill.
SUMMER: crested tit, crossbill, siskin, capercaillie, black grouse, golden eagle, woodcock, greenshank, willow and wood warblers, redstart, carrion and hooded crows.

The Spey is flanked on the west by the A9 and on the east by the B970 and there are railway stations at Aviemore and Kincraig. The whole area is comparatively open and free of access though it is advisable to keep to the established tracks wherever possible. These are numerous out of the Aviemore–Coylumbridge area and from the shore of Loch Morlich. Places worth visiting include Loch an Eilean where the castle is an old and famous osprey haunt; Loch Morlich where ospreys regularly fish; and a walk through the heart of Rothiemurchus. The Forestry Commission publishes a booklet of 'Walks in the Queen's Forest' dealing with Glenmore Forest Park.

As a growing resort the area is well served by hotels. See Map, page 158.

Speyside: showing the three important forest areas of Rothiemurchus, Glen More, and Abernethy. Loch Garten is the breeding haunt of ospreys and Loch Morlich a favourite fishing ground, while Loch an Eilean is a celebrated nineteenth-century haunt. Glen More is an excellent centre and has a Youth Hostel and camp site

TIREE (Argyll)   OS 44

Tiree lies in the Inner Hebrides immediately west of Mull. It is
however, not protected from the Atlantic by the Outer
Hebrides and so receives the full force of gales. Because of this
it has a landscape closely akin to that of the outer islands with
extensive beaches of shell sand and a generally fertile mixture
of sand and peat, whereas Coll, its easterly neighbour, is sheltered from the ocean and is to a large extent bare rock and
peat. Wildfowl find the island attractive and Loch a' Phuill and
Loch Bhasapoll are major centres, though white-fronts are
found on the Reef, a marshy area in the centre of the island.
Sea duck are numerous in the bays, and Gunna between Tiree
and Coll, holds 400 barnacle geese. The vast beaches hold
waders on passage and the island is renowned as the best snipe
shooting in Europe! The cliffs at Ceann a'Mhara in the south-
west hold breeding sea birds, and Gunna has terns.

Nearby Coll holds Arctic skua and red-throated diver.

WINTER: wigeon, gadwall, tufted duck, goldeneye, eider,
merganser, barnacle and white-fronted geese, snipe, jack
snipe.
SPRING: whimbrel, turnstone, sanderling.
SUMMER: common and Arctic terns, ringed plover, guillemot,
razorbill, black guillemot, red-throated diver, wheatear,
stonechat, hooded crow, Arctic skua.
AUTUMN: bar-tailed godwit, sanderling, greenshank.

MacBraynes' steamers leave Oban 3 days a week to Coll and
Tiree. Return fare to the latter is 31s. second class. Tiree has
an airport and there are frequent services from Glasgow. A
range of accommodation is available – but book in advance.
There are hotels at Arinagour on Coll and Scarinish on Tiree.

WEST LOCH TARBERT (Argyll)   OS 58

This is a 10 mile long sea loch that almost separates Kintyre
from the mainland. Because of its geographical position it is
used as the major shipping route between Glasgow and the
Highlands by MacBraynes with a shuttle bus service between it
and East Loch Tarbert. Its convenience as a transport centre
makes the winter concentrations of sea duck, grebes, and especially great northern divers easily accessible. A flock of white-
fronts winters on the flats opposite Gigha, and numbers of barnacles are noted at the loch mouth in spring.

WINTER: great northern diver, Slavonian grebe, velvet scoter,
eider, long-tailed duck, white-fronted goose.
SPRING: barnacle goose.

Frequent steamers from Gourock to Tarbert and coaches on the A83 along the southern side of the loch. Alternatively, and better, explore by car. The steamer trip to Gigha and back is outstanding.

Ayrshire, Dunbartonshire, Lanarkshire, Renfrewshire and Stirlingshire

AILSA CRAIG (Ayr)   OS 72

A precipitous hump in the Firth of Clyde threequarters of a mile long and rising to 1,110 feet. It lies 10 miles west of Girvan and is quarried commercially. Ailsa is one of Britain's foremost sea bird breeding stations. Recent counts suggest that about 13,500 pairs of gannets breed, together with large numbers of the commoner species, including both northern and southern guillemots.

SUMMER: gannet, razorbill, guillemot, puffin, kittiwake.

A boat leaves Girvan harbour every Monday and Friday, cost 20s., to land and take off quarrymen; this trip does *not* allow sufficient time to visit the sea bird colonies. However it is possible to camp on the island with the permission of Mr. I. Girvan, 'Millcraig', Henrietta Street, Girvan, who is also the boatman. Other boats make trips during summer allowing other camping arrangements – but time does not permit a worthwhile exploration without staying overnight. Consult the Publicity Department, Town Clerk's Office, Girvan.

British Railways run a steamer trip round the island three times each summer and this gives good views not normally available from small boats.

Under no circumstances should the gannetry be closely approached after 15 July. By this date the young birds are well grown and tend to leave their nests at human approach. Such action is inevitably fatal.

GRANGEMOUTH (Stirling)   OS 61; HT + 0:30 Leith

Grangemouth lies on the southern shore of the Forth above Edinburgh. Between Kincardine Bridge and Bo'ness the mud-flats are up to $1\frac{1}{2}$ miles wide and are interrupted only by the Grangemouth Docks extension. Though this central area is an industrial sprawl the birds are outstanding. Wildfowl usually number several thousand and include roosting greylags and pinkfeet, December–March. Vast numbers of knot are present with other waders in winter when the main roosts are at Longannet Point and Kincardine Bridge on the Fife shore. The present industrial developments on both sites will doubtless change this situation. In autumn a large range of waders pass through including most of the fresh species, especially at Skinflats to the west of Grangemouth. High tide visits advised.

WINTER: wigeon, pintail, goldeneye, goosander, merganser, shelduck, greylag and pink-footed geese, knot, bar-tailed godwit, turnstone, merlin.

SPRING: waders.

AUTUMN: knot, bar-tailed godwit, whimbrel, curlew sandpiper, little stint, green sandpiper, spotted redshank, grey plover, ruff.

The dockland area of Grangemouth provides excellent, if unsavoury, views over large areas of mud. Leave the town centre northwards up the eastern side of the docks.

For Skinflats, leave Grangemouth northwards on the A905, cross the River Carron and take the first turning right past Skinflats village. Continue on one of several tracks to the sea wall.

LENZIE LOCH (Gadloch) (Lanark)   OS 60

The loch is 4 miles north-east of central Glasgow and immediately south of Lenzie. Its western banks consist of mudflats in summer made up of coal silt brought down by a stream from a nearby pit. Wildfowl are the most interesting birds especially in spring and autumn, though up to 300 greylags are resident in winter. The coal mudflats attract waders on passage and eighteen species have been reported to date.

WINTER: greylag goose, wigeon, teal, golden plover.

SPRING: whooper swan, geese, duck, waders.

SUMMER: pochard.

AUTUMN: wildfowl, green sandpiper, snipe, spotted redshank.

Leave Glasgow northwards on the A803 and turn right after 4 miles on to the B819. The loch is on the right after 2 miles. It is surrounded by farmland but can be seen from the road at many points at distances down to 50 yards.

LOCH LOMOND (Dunbarton/Stirling)   OS 53

Loch Lomond lies north-west of Glasgow and is a wonderful, open playground for the people of the industrial lowlands. It is an extremely beautiful area and the lochside and many islands are well wooded with semi-natural oaks and recent conifers. Though mergansers and capercaillie breed and the woodlands hold the usual highland summer species, the main attraction is the wildfowl in winter. These concentrate around the mouth of the Endrick in the south east which is now part of a National Nature Reserve covering 624 acres. Duck are numerous and greylags number 1,000. White-fronts and pinkfeet are occasional but the once regular bean geese have now disappeared. Waders are regular on passage.

WINTER: wigeon, shoveler, pochard, tufted duck, merganser, goldeneye, greylag and white fronted geese, whooper swan.
SUMMER: merganser, redstart, grey wagtail, grasshopper and other warblers.
AUTUMN: black-tailed godwit, waders.

Leave Glasgow northwards on the A809. Turn left on to the B837 at Drymen and continue to Balmaha. Access is restricted in parts of the reserve and permission is required to visit these and to camp. All inquiries to Nature Conservancy Scottish Office or the Warden, Mr. Idle at 22 Muirpark Way, Drymen. Arrangements to visit the islands can be made at the boat house, Balmaha.

Berwickshire, The Lothians (East, West and Mid), Peeblesshire, Roxburghshire and Selkirkshire

ABERLADY BAY (East Lothian)
OS 62; HT −0:11 Leith

This is a tidal estuary lying north of Aberlady Village on the A198 between Edinburgh and North Berwick. Its 1,400 acres of foreshore and dunes have been made a local nature reserve. Several hundred duck use the bay and pinkfeet are frequently present. Waders include the usual species in winter and a wider variety on passage, especially autumn. Aberlady is the most regular place in Scotland for wood sandpipers.

Gullane Point on the northern side of the bay is an excellent place for sea birds, notably red-necked grebes, at all seasons.

WINTER: pink-footed goose, wigeon, scoter, velvet scoter, merganser, long-tailed duck, knot, bar-tailed godwit, red-necked grebe, divers.
SPRING: waders, red-necked grebe, divers.
SUMMER: long-eared owl, common, Arctic and little terns, dunlin, redshank,
AUTUMN: skuas, terns, green, wood and curlew sandpipers, grey plover, black-tailed godwit, little stint, ruff, red-necked, black-necked and Slavonian grebes, divers.

Leave Aberlady eastwards and stop at the head of the bay where a timber bridge crosses the small stream. There are no limitations on access except to a small part in summer.

BASS ROCK (East Lothian)   OS 56

Bass Rock lies 1½ miles offshore and 3 miles north-east of
Berwick at the mouth of the Firth of Forth. It is a quarter of a
mile by 300 yards and is a large gannetry. Nearly 6,000 breeding pairs were counted in a recent survey.

SUMMER: gannet, fulmar, shag, kittiwake, guillemot, razorbill, puffin.

Access is by permission of the owner and by boat from
North Berwick. The Scottish Ornithologists' Club run
organised excursions most summers. Because of the risk of
disturbance to this valuable sanctuary, all visitors should in-
quire first to the Scottish Ornithologists' Club. North Berwick boatmen do trips round the island that give excellent
views.

CHEVIOT Hills (Roxburgh)   OS 70 and 71

The Cheviots form the border between England and Scotland
and rise to 2,676 feet. The vast area of heather and grass moorland is as lonely as any could wish and does not even attract
climbers, walkers and tourists to any great extent. The hills
have been long famous as a haunt of birds, including the usual
moorland species. Almost every plantation holds woodcock,
and black grouse are numerous.

SUMMER: golden plover, dunlin, woodcock, merlin, short-
eared owl, ring ouzel, dipper, red grouse, black grouse.

There are several roads leading into the heart of the hills,
notably on the northern and eastern sides. All are public except that from Westnewton up the College Valley on the
northern side, 1 mile west of Kirknewton on the B6351. Permission to motor up must be obtained from D. M. Campbell,
Estate Agent, Wooler. Wooler is a good centre with accommodation and good roads up Harthope Burn. There are footpaths throughout the area and no restrictions on the open
moor.

DUDDINGSTON LOCH (Mid-Lothian)   OS 62

This is a natural loch lying within 1½ miles of the centre of
Edinburgh and extending to 30 acres including a large reed
bed. Since 1925 the area has been a nature reserve, belonging
to the Ministry of Works. The loch is used by over 700 duck
in winter and a few waders appear on passage.

WINTER: wigeon, shoveler, tufted duck, pochard, goldeneye,
water rail, great crested grebe, corn bunting.

SUMMER: great crested grebe, little grebe, tufted duck,

pochard, long-eared owl, sedge warbler, whitethroat, willow warbler, reed bunting.

Access is prohibited but the reserve can be overlooked from many points on the roads in Holyrood Park and excellent views obtained from Duddingston Foreshore where the loch meets the park close to Duddingston Road on the north bank.

FIDRA, EYEBROUGHTY AND THE LAMB
(East Lothian)   OS 56

These are three small rocky islets lying less than a mile off the East Lothian shore of the Firth of Forth and covering a total of 6 acres. Fidra is the largest and supports breeding colonies of terns, including a few pairs of roseate. The Lamb has the only colony of cormorants in the Forth, and Eyebroughty is the smallest island and mainly noted as a moulting ground for up to 2,000 eiders in June and July.

SUMMER: common, Arctic, Sandwich and roseate terns, cormorant, shag, eider, kittiwake, fulmar, gulls.

The islands are managed as reserves by the RSPB and arrangements to land should be made through the Society's Scottish Office, 21 Regent Terrace, Edinburgh 7. To see the moulting eiders from the mainland, leave the A198 at the eastern end of Dirleton village northwards to Yellowcraig car park. Walk along the coast $1\frac{1}{2}$ miles westwards. The shore opposite Fidra is a good place to see roseates without getting into a boat.

GLADHOUSE RESERVOIR (Mid-Lothian)   OS 62

The reservoir lies in the Moorfoot Hills 13 miles south of Edinburgh at 900 feet and covers 400 acres. The water is a major roost of greylag (1,000) and pink-feet (8,000) from October to December, and is then used again in the spring. Gulls, too, use it as a secure base. Snow buntings are regular and the passage of waders is excellent for an inland locality.

WINTER: pink-footed and greylag geese, wigeon, teal, tufted duck, golden-eye, goosander, gulls, snow bunting.

SPRING: waders.

SUMMER: duck, grasshopper warbler, black grouse.

AUTUMN: greenshank, oystercatcher, ruff, green sandpiper.

Leave Edinburgh south-eastwards on the A7 and turn right on to the B6372 just past Gorebridge. Follow this past Rosebery Reservoir on the left and where the road turns sharp right take the half left up to the fir wood. Turn sharp left on emerging and view the reservoir round the north-western side. Access is strictly prohibited, and trespassers are doing bird-watching a great deal of harm.

INCHMICKERY (Mid-Lothian)   OS 62

This is an island lying in the middle of the Firth of Forth about
4 miles from the centre of Edinburgh. It covers 3 acres and was
heavily built up by the military occupation of 1939. Its colony
of 450 pairs of roseate terns is the largest in the Forth and
other terns breed in good numbers.

SUMMER: roseate, common, Arctic and Sandwich terns.

The island is an RSPB reserve and access is by permit obtainable from the Society's Scottish Office, 21 Regent Terrace,
Edinburgh 7. A boat costs £2–£5 according to the number of
visitors.

ST. ABB'S HEAD (Berwick)   OS 64

St. Abb's Head is on the coast 12 miles north of Berwick-upon-
Tweed. Though the cliffs at the Head rise to over 300 feet they
stretch westwards almost to Cockburnspath and reach a maximum height of 500 feet. Breeding sea birds are the main
interest, including a small number of puffins, and there are 8
miles of cliff to explore.

SUMMER: razorbill, guillemot, puffin, kittiwake, fulmar.

Several tracks leave the A1107 eastwards between Cock-
burnspath and Coldingham that lead to the cliff top. That to
Dowlaw is easy to find and has a footpath at the end over
Telegraph Hill to Fast Castle which is a good spot.

SEAFIELD, LEITH (Mid-Lothian)   OS 62; HT at Leith

Seafield consists of a long sea wall to the east of Leith Docks
with some sandy shores further east. There is a sewage outfall
that attracts vast numbers of sea duck in winter and numerous
other species at all seasons. Scaup, up to 10,000, are dominant
but other large numbers include 2,000 goldeneye, 1,500 scoter,
and hundreds of eider and long-tailed duck. Up to 400 great
crested grebe have been counted and large numbers of mergansers congregate at the mouth of the Esk at Musselburgh in
autumn. On passage many species are noted.

WINTER: scaup, scoter, eider, long-tailed duck, great crested
grebe, knot.

SPRING: waders, terns.

AUTUMN: gannet, waders, terns, skuas.

Take the bus from Leith to Portobello and alight at Seafield.
Cross the railway to the north.

TYNE MOUTH (East Lothian)   OS 63; HT —0:08 Leith

The rivermouth lies immediately west of Dunbar and forms a small estuary 1½ miles by half a mile. It has areas of saltings and holds up to 1,000 pink-feet and the odd greylag and brent. Duck are both numerous and varied and the usual estuary waders winter and are augmented by passage species.

WINTER: pink-footed goose, wigeon, shelduck, goldeneye, eider, waders.

SPRING: green sandpiper.

SUMMER: eider, shelduck, ringed plover, short-eared owl.

AUTUMN: green and curlew sandpipers, ruff, whimbrel, greenshank, little stint.

Leave Dunbar westwards on the A1087. Turn northwards in West Barns and follow footpath along the south side of estuary. The reefs offshore are a daytime roost of wildfowl. For the north side, continue on the A1087, turn right on to the A198 and half a mile past Tyninghame village turn right again. Park at car park and continue down track to the sea. The surrounding estate is strictly private.

Tyne Mouth: an attractive wooded tidal basin with private land on all sides

Caithness, Ross, Cromarty and Sutherland

Inverness is over 500 miles north of London, and Caithness and the north coast lie in the same latitude as southern Norway.

The land, which is predominantly deer forest, with its covering of poor grasses and cotton-sedge bogs, is sparsely inhabited and bird-watchers can walk for days without meeting anyone but the odd stalker. Accommodation is difficult and in many places impossible. Enthusiasts looking for the unusual birds that breed will do well to bring their own accommodation plus a large stock of food. It has a bird population distinctly different from England much closer to that of Scandinavia. The crows are hooded, the nuthatch unknown, and the common bird around the dwellings is the twite.

The specialities of the area are mainly birds connected with water and include black-throated and red-throated divers, greylag goose, wigeon, merganser, scoter, various waders, Slavonian grebe, skuas and golden eagle. Sporadic breeders include scaup, snow bunting, redwing and brambling. Much of Sutherland is still poorly known and even holiday notes can be useful.

Transport is by car or foot. Boats can usually be obtained to visit any island but are expensive unless a group shares the fare.

BEAULY FIRTH (Ross & Cromarty)

OS 28; HT at Inverness

Beauly Firth lies at the head of the Moray Firth system. The western end consists of extensive saltings and mud banks, along the southern shore, and is a favourite haunt of duck. Pink-feet top 500 in spring and greylag are particularly numerous in autumn. At this time herring shoals enter the firth and an array of predators gather at Kessock. These include up to 400 each of merganser and goosander with frequently large numbers of kittiwakes.

WINTER: wigeon, pintail, greylag goose.
SPRING: pink-footed goose, waders.
SUMMER: shelduck, merganser, black-headed gull.
AUTUMN: Canada goose, merganser, goosander, kittiwake, bar-tailed godwit, greenshank, grey plover.

Leave Beauly eastwards on the A9 and view from convenient lay-bys. Or leave northwards and turn right at Muir of Ord on to the A832. After 2¼ miles turn right to Redcastle and continue along northern shore to North Kessock.

CLO MOR (Sutherland)

OS 9

Clo Mor lies on the north coast of Sutherland, 4 miles east of

Cape Wrath and form the highest cliffs on the British mainland. They are renowed for outstanding colonies of sea birds. Ptarmigan breed at an extremely low level and at Cape Wrath a main attraction is the almost constant stream of gannets offshore.

SUMMER: guillemot, razorbill, puffin, black guillemot, gannet, fulmar, peregrine, golden eagle, ptarmigan.

Leave the A838 alongside the Kyle of Durness to Keoldale. The ferry across the Kyle costs 3s. 6d. return, and Paul Brown's minibus runs up to Cape Wrath at 12s. 6d. return. Access is prohibited when the area is used as a naval artillery range which is sometimes for 2 or 3 weeks in summer, but limited access to Cape Wrath lighthouse is allowed at certain hours.

Accommodation is very difficult in summer. Kyle and Glen Highland Safaris include visits to the area in their Sutherland weeks.

CROMARTY FIRTH (Ross & Cromarty)
                              OS 22 and 28; HT −0:37 Inverness

This is an 18 mile long inlet varying between 1 mile and 5 miles wide with huge bays and areas of sand and mud. The head of the firth around Dingwall has saltings and a huge expanse of foreshore holding very little but a few duck, waders and up to 500 greylags. At Invergordon there are concentrations of gulls, duck and mute swans feeding on the waste outflow from a distillery. Udale Bay on the southern shore holds the best collection of birds on the estuary, including good numbers of passage waders. The Sutors rise to over 450 feet on either side of the entrance and the cliffs on the northern side hold fulmar and cormorant.

WINTER: wigeon, goldeneye, merganser, greylag goose, knot, bar-tailed godwit, turnstone, grey plover.

SPRING: waders.

SUMMER: fulmar, cormorant.

AUTUMN: whimbrel, greenshank, turnstone, knot.

Leave Dingwall northwards and view from the A9 which leads to Invergordon for the distillery. From here there is a foot ferry to the south shore and a good track via Newhallpoint to Udale Bay. The B9163 leads along the north side of Black Isle to the bay. For the North Sutor leave the A9 southeastwards 2¼ miles north of Kildary and follow lanes through Castlecraig.

DORNOCH FIRTH (Ross & Cromarty)
                              OS 22; HT +0:43 Inverness

The inner firth beyond Dornoch Point is over 12 miles long and contains a number of the most outstanding bird resorts in Scotland. At the entrance on the southern side there is the expanse of Morrich More with its dune slacks and extensive salt-marsh. Behind the More lies Loch Eye over 1½ miles long and outstanding in its own right. And to the north is Tarbat Ness, an excellent place for a sea watch. The cliffs south of Rockfield on the eastern side of the Tarbat peninsula hold fulmars.

Tarbat Ness is a useful place to go after a day around the estuary. In spring large numbers of long tailed duck congregate here and in autumn shearwaters, skuas and purple sandpipers can be seen.

From Whiteness Point to Edderton the sandy foreshore is hardly less than 1 mile wide and is the resort of hordes of wildfowl. Geese are most plentiful in spring and autumn and the only flock of white-fronts in east Scotland occurs in March. The roost of these birds is on Morrich More which is used as a military firing range. This is also the roost of the largest flocks of waders in north-east Scotland.

Loch Eye holds most of the wildfowl species found on the estuary, and in autumn fresh waders are excellent. The only other place on the southern shores is the fresh water pool enclosed by the railway at Fearn. This is a notable resort of whooper swans in winter and waders on passage.

On the northern shore the sands at Dornoch and Cuthill hold duck and the usual waders. While to the west, the muddy Skibo Inlet and the adjacent Loch Evelix provide a resort for duck and whooper swan.

The firth is well worth a visit at any season but is outstanding in autumn.

WINTER: greylag goose, wigeon, pintail, teal, scaup, tufted duck, pochard, whooper swan, knot, bar-tailed godwit, divers.

SPRING: greylag, pink-footed and white-fronted geese, knot, bar-tailed godwit, grey plover, turnstone, purple sandpiper.

SUMMER: fulmar, terns, waders.

AUTUMN: greylag and pink-footed geese, wigeon, knot, bar-tailed godwit, whimbrel, turnstone, sanderling, greenshank, grey plover, purple sandpiper.

Access to all points is directly from the A9 which runs along the north and south shores:

1. TARBAT NESS: leave the A9 3 miles south of Tain on to the B9165.
2. TAIN: bridge over the railway west of the station.

3. EDDERTON SANDS: leave A9 3 miles west of Tain north-wards to Ferry Point.

4. FEARN POOL: alongside A9 between Easter and Wester Fearn.

5. SKIBO INLET: leave the A9 southwards at Clashmore and turn right at T-junction to Ferrytown.

6. CUTHILL-DORNOCH SANDS: at T-junction in 5 continue on track across Cuthill Links. Access to Dornoch Point via golf course and municipal camping site.

LOCH FLEET (Sutherland)   OS 22; HT−0:30 Inverness

The loch lies on the east coast and is a virtually land-locked basin 3 miles by 1 mile. At low tide it is almost totally dry providing a fine habitat for waders and wildfowl. Attempts to reclaim the upper estuary by building an embankment called The Mound in 1815 were only partially successful. The 2 miles above The Mound are now a dense alder swamp giving shelter to a variety of breeding birds. The fresh water pool is a favourite haunt of many species. Mergansers reach a high peak in autumn and waders are plentiful in winter and are joined by the usual array on passage. Eiders are particularly numerous at the mouth and now breed amongst the dunes in Ferry Links. Both scoter and velvet scoter winter off Embo in rafts of up to 1,000, and long-tailed duck gather in Golspie Bay.

WINTER: wigeon, teal, goldeneye, scoter, velvet scoter, eider, long-tailed duck, knot.

SPRING: shelduck, waders.

SUMMER: eider.

AUTUMN: knot, greenshank, turnstone, merganser, eider.

Leave Dornoch westwards on the B9168 forking right outside the town. Join the A9 and immediately fork right on to the unclassified road to Skelbo. Continue over the railway to the pier. Leave Skelbo westwards along the southern shore, join the A9 and cross The Mound.

HANDA ISLAND (Sutherland)   OS 9

The island lies half a mile offshore 3 miles north-west of Scourie on the west coast of Sutherland, and is an RSPB reserve. The island covers 766 acres with 400 foot cliffs, sandy beaches, moorlands and lochs. The cliffs hold 25,000 pairs of guillemots and lesser numbers of the other auks and cliff-nesters. A wide variety of other species breed or can be seen in summer.

SUMMER: razorbill, guillemot, puffin, kittiwake, fulmar, eider, Arctic tern, rock dove, twite, skuas.

Day visitors do not require permits and landings can be arranged with the Warden, A. Munro, Tarbert, Foindle, by Lairg. There is a reconditioned bothy which accommodates 8 people on a hostel basis and bookings for this should be made with the RSPB Scottish Office.

Accommodation is limited, there is a small hotel in Scourie, but Kyle and Glen Minicoaches include Handa in many of their holidays.

INVERPOLLY (Sutherland)   OS 13

This area is a National Nature Reserve covering 26,827 acres of the wildest and remotest country in Britain. It includes high summits, streams, moorland, cliffs and woodland, and, lying on Lewisian Gneiss, is very wet and boggy with innumerable lakes. Though primarily of interest to geologists, bearing some of the oldest rock in the world, the area around Elphin and Knockan, is limestone and is a green and fertile jewel amongst the wild surrounding landscape. The centre of the Reserve is the large Loch Sionascaig. Wild cats and pine martens are the mammal stars but breeding birds are excellent.

SUMMER: black-throated diver, black guillemot, merganser, ptarmigan, raven, golden eagle, buzzard, stonechat, ring ouzel.

Permission is required from The Warden, Strathpolly, Inverpolly, by Ullapool; and from Assynt Estate Office, Lochinver for parties of more than 6 and for any visit between 15 July and 15 October. Leave the A835 by Old Drumrunie Lodge westwards. After 4 miles a footpath on the right runs to the centre of the Reserve. A track leads off to the right to Inverpolly in a further 5 miles. Approaching from the north, leave Lochinver southwards to Inverkirkaig, pass through the village and park at the bridge. Continue up the southern bank of the River Kirkaig.

Accommodation is limited.

KYLE OF TONGUE AND ROAN ISLAND (Sutherland)
                              OS 10; HT+1:00 Stornoway

Situated on the north Sutherland coast, the Kyle is a long tidal inlet with extensive mud banks for most of its length. It holds numbers of waders on passage, but is not outstanding for wildfowl though a number of species breed in the neighbourhood. Roan Island, or correctly, Eilean nan Ron, lies at the entrance to the estuary and held a small human population until 1938. It is mainly noted as the winter haunt of up to 200 barnacle geese, often 300 in spring; but is also a good summer spot for breeding birds. Tongue village has a rookery, the most northerly on the British mainland.

WINTER: barnacle goose.

SUMMER: duck, rook, storm petrel, fulmar, peregrine, kittiwake, common and Arctic terns, black guillemot, rock dove.

AUTUMN: waders.

The wintering barnacles can be seen from the adjacent mainland with a telescope. Trips to the island are by private charter at Tongue or Skerray.

Tongue Pier is a good vantage point for the estuary and the A838 runs down the western shore extended northwards by an unclassified road.

Accommodation is limited but there is a Youth Hostel at Tongue.

NOSS HEAD (Caithness)   OS 16

The head stands 3 miles north of Wick on the east coast. Its cliffs barely reach 100 feet but are good for breeding sea birds and for sea watching.

SUMMER: guillemot, razorbill, black guillemot, puffin, kittiwake, fulmar.

Leave Wick northwards on the unclassified road across the airport. There are sometimes delays here due to aircraft movements but they are never prolonged. Walk westward from the lighthouse over boggy fields to Sinclair Castle.

SUMMER ISLES (Ross & Cromarty)   OS 13

The islands lie at the mouth of Loch Broom and are a notable bird haunt. 300 barnacle geese winter on Glas Leac Beag which is the summer haunt of large gull colonies. It is also the island chosen as the moulting ground of the Summer Isles greylags in July and August. The major island and the one most likely to be visited is Tanera More which holds greylag, red-throated diver, Arctic tern and buzzard, while the smaller Carn non Sgeir, which is en route to Tanera More, holds black guillemot and eider. Storm petrels breed on Priest Island.

WINTER: barnacle goose.

SUMMER: greylag goose, storm petrel, red-throated diver, Arctic tern, black guillemot, eider, rock dove, buzzard, heron.

Boats run quite frequently from Ullapool, Mr. Macrae, Beach House; and Achiltibuie, Mr. Macleod, Post Office. Time ashore is limited unless the boat is chartered.

Dumfriesshire, Kirkcudbrightshire, Wigtownshire (Solway)

CAERLAVEROCK (Dumfries)

OS 75; HT+1:10 Liverpool

Caerlaverock, on the northern shore of the Solway, is one of the most outstanding bird haunts in Britain. The area treated here stretches from the Nith to the mouth of the Lochar Water. Throughout this length the Merse salt marsh is anything up to a mile wide and inter-tidal mud stretches out into the estuary for another 3 miles. The eastern third of the Merse, covering 13,514 acres, was established as Caerlaverock National Nature Reserve in 1957 and is one of the principal haunts of barnacle geese in Britain. Up to 2,800 have been recorded. This number is totally dwarfed, however, by the 10,000–12,000 pink-feet that arrive in autumn and the 10,000 that winter. Greylag geese number 1,000 in winter with 2,000 in spring, and waders are plentiful. Autumn brings the best collection of waders on the Scottish west coast.

WINTER: barnacle, pink-footed and greylag geese, whooper swan, wigeon, pintail, knot, hen harrier, peregrine, merlin.
SPRING: greylag goose, waders.
AUTUMN: pink-footed goose, black-tailed godwit.

Access to Caerlaverock National Nature Reserve is usually only granted on Sundays and then by prior arrangement with the Warden, Mr. E. L. Roberts, Tadorna, Hollands Farm Road, Caerlaverock, by Dumfries.

There are, however, several public roads which, with the 7 miles of the B725, make observation of all species straightforward without disturbing the Reserve at all. Indeed the best place for whooper swans is the Nith above Glencaple.

View from any point on the B725 between Kelton and the wood south of Caerlaverock Castle, the track south of this wood continues these views eastwards. Further east there are decent views from the road again at the mouth of the Lochar water near Stanhope. See Map page 174.

DEE VALLEY (Kirkcudbright)

OS 73, 74, 80 and 81

The entire length of the valley between Castle Douglas and New Galloway, a distance something over 12 miles, is worth exploring. Greylag (600), white-fronted (500), pink-footed (200) and bean-geese (50) are all present, though the latter are fast declining.

Dumfries—Kircudbright: showing Caerlaverock National Nature Reserve and Southerness Point and the vast wildfowl haunt between the two. Most of the area can be worked from classified roads

The major area of interest in the valley lies above the hydro-electricity dam near Townhead of Greenlaw. Loch Ken is up to half a mile wide in places and provides one of the most important roosts in the area. The marshes below the dam at Threave, together with Carlingwark Loch outside Castle Douglas are important areas.

The whole is best treated in three parts:

1. CASTLE DOUGLAS–THREAVE: this is the main area for the bean geese, with greylags numerous and a few white-fronts. It also holds the largest numbers of duck. Carlingwark Loch is a shallow pool of 105 acres and holds large numbers of diving duck. Whooper swans are regular.

2. THE RIVER DEE up to 1 mile north of Crossmichael: greylag and white-fronts frequent this area with quite good numbers of duck on the wider part above Livingston.

3. LOCH KEN: begins properly above the Loch Ken viaduct. There is a larger area of open water in this part which, together with the marsh at the head of the loch, attract numbers of duck and some white-fronts.

WINTER: greylag, white-fronted, pink-footed and bean geese, whooper swan, wigeon, pintail, shoveler, goldeneye, gadwall, smew.

SPRING AND AUTUMN: wildfowl.

The three areas are reached as follows:

1. CARLINGWARK LOCH can be seen from the A75 south of Castle Douglas but the geese move around the area so much that a general exploration to the south-east and north-west of the town is recommended. The Threave marshes can be penetrated from the A75, but the road to Netherhall north from Bridge of Dee repays investigation.

2. Leave the A713 westwards at Townhead of Greenlaw. Cross the dam on the B795 and turn right immediately. This unclassified road gives excellent views for 2 miles to Livingston.

3. LOCH KEN: the A762 runs alongside the Loch for the top 4 miles including the marshy north end, and the A713 gives more intermittent views from the east bank.

All of these areas contain valuable farm land and watchers should not enter fields or disturb stock without permission. Many farmers dislike the geese and carelessness or lack of understanding of other interests by bird-watchers will make things worse for the birds in the end. Generally satisfactory views can be obtained from public roads without disturbing either farmers or geese.

LOCHMABEN (Dumfries) OS 75

This is a small town 10 miles east of Dumfries on the A709. It is a good wildfowl centre with large numbers of duck on the surrounding lochs and along the meandering course of the River Annan where there are numerous floods and oxbow lakes. The most important area is Castle Loch which covers

210 acres and holds up to 1,000 greylag geese. Part of the area, including Castle Loch, is a local nature reserve.

WINTER: greylag goose, wigeon, shoveler, pochard, goosander.

Castle Loch lies alongside the A709 south of Lochmaben. Views can also be obtained from the western side from the B7020. Kirk Loch and Mill Loch can be seen from public roads ref. OS 75.

The Annan meadows and floods are the major feeding ground of the geese and a search is often necessary. The bridge over the river on the A709 is a useful vantage point looking south, and there are several unclassified roads running north and south along both sides of the river.

MILTON LOCH (Kirkcudbright)   OS 74

The loch is about a mile south of the A75 between Dumfries and Castle Douglas. It is perhaps the best of a number of good places in the neighbourhood for wildfowl, which include Lochrutton Loch and Auchenreoch Loch. Milton Loch, less than a mile long, holds 300 greylag geese and up to 1,000 duck.

WINTER: greylag goose, teal, wigeon.

Take the A75 from either Dumfries or Castle Douglas and turn southwards at Ninemile Bar just west of its junction with the A712. Fork left in three-quarters of a mile and view from the road in a further three-quarters of a mile.

PRIESTSIDE BANK (Dumfries)
                              OS 75; HT+0:30 Liverpool

This spot is the easternmost of the main geese resorts on the Scottish shore of the Solway, and is separated from the huge Blackshaw Bank off Caerlaverock by the channel of the Lochar Water. A narrow strip of merse lies between the flat lowland and the huge banks. Pink-feet are often very numerous and greylags can usually be seen, with, sometimes, a flock of barnacles. Duck are not notable but like the waders are regularly present in numbers.

WINTER: pink-footed, greylag and barnacle geese, wigeon, pintail, waders, peregrine, merlin.

Leave Annan westwards on the A75, cross the river and in 600 yards turn left on to the B724. Turn left after 3½ miles in Cummertrees and after 1 mile a track leads down to the shore.

SOUTHERNESS POINT (Kirkcudbright)
                              OS 75; HT+0:30 Liverpool

The point juts out into the Solway to the west of the Nith.

Though the flatness of the area is reminiscent of other marshes it is the rocky foreshore and the sea that provide the main attractions. The sea often holds vast flocks of sea duck and, in the last two Februarys, a few surf scoter.

WINTER: scoter, velvet scoter, scaup, merganser, surf scoter, great crested grebe, red-throated diver, purple sandpiper, turnstone, knot, bar-tailed godwit.

Leave the A710 by any one of three unclassified roads south of Kirkbean and follow through to Southerness Point. See Map, page 174.

WIGTOWN BAY (Kirkcudbright/Wigtown)
OS 80; HT+0:19 Liverpool

A vast area of inter-tidal sands stretching 7 miles from Spital to the mouth at Jultock Point and up to 3 miles across. The upper estuary in particular has large expanses of merse salt marsh, and the 2 square miles of the Moss of Cree lie immediately inland. The area attracts a wintering flock of up to 2,500 greylags which are joined in March by 2,000 pink-feet. The level of duck is high with total reaching several thousand every winter. An unusual occurrence is the flock of up to 2,000 scoter that assemble at the mouth of the bay in late July. The waders are the usual and sometimes very numerous.

WINTER: greylag goose, wigeon, pintail, shoveler, shelduck, whooper swan, waders.

SPRING: pink-footed goose.

SUMMER: scoter.

The main area for wildfowl is the western shore which is particularly difficult of access. On the eastern side, the A75 gives good views over the entire estuary at many points and particularly at Creetown and Spital. An unclassified road running north from Wigtown between the estuary and the Moss of Cree offers the best chance of observation on that side.

Orkney Islands

The Orkneys are separated from Caithness by the Pentland Firth which is at one point no more than 6 miles wide. There are 29 inhabited isles, 38 holmes, and a vast number of skerries. The landscape is generally low and rolling though Hoy rises to over 1,500 feet, and has fine cliffs and stacks. It is basically an agricultural land with a large number of small farmers. There are extensive lochs and a considerable area of damp moorland. Its sea bird cliffs are excellent, especially on Hoy and many divers and waders breed around its inland lochs. The red-necked phalarope still breeds on one island and both skuas are increasing and spreading.

The islands have long been famous as the stronghold of the hen harrier, and due in no small measure to the work of the RSPB Representative, E. Balfour, they have increased and spread back to the Scottish mainland.

LOCH OF HARRAY AND LOCH OF STENNESS
OS 6

These two lochs lie in the south-west of the mainland north of Stromness and are linked in the south-east. Though Stenness joins the sea it can only be called brackish, while Harray is all but fresh. Their summer population includes a wide variety of breeding wildfowl and other species. In winter both lochs are excellent for wildfowl, with the sea duck on Stenness and the others on Harray.

WINTER: scaup, long-tailed duck, goldeneye, pochard, tufted duck, whooper and mute swans.

SUMMER: dunlin, common gull, eider, merganser, tufted duck, common tern.

The A965 from Stromness leads to the B9055 which runs between the lochs giving access to both. Boats for hire are available at different places, and Harray is noted for trout.

HOY
OS 7

Hoy is the most westerly island of the Orkney group, the second largest, being 14 miles by 6 miles, and scenically the most varied, rising to over 1,500 feet and exposing an extensive line of cliffs on the western coast. These culminate in the Old Man of Hoy, a noted tourist spot, and hold numerous colonies of sea birds. Manx shearwaters breed in the north. The hills hold Arctic and great skuas.

SUMMER: guillemot, razorbill, puffin, kittiwake, fulmar, raven, Arctic and great skuas, Manx shearwater, red-throated diver.

Hoy is reached by the motor vessels of the Bremner Shipping Co., which sail from Stromness to Longhope 3 days per week throughout the year; and almost daily in the summer, the fare is 11s. 0d. A hostel has been created from the old school at Rackwick on the west coast and accommodation is available at 3s. 6d. per night. Inquiries and booking to the Orkney County Youth Leader, Education Officer, Kirkwall. Bremner also call at Graemsay, Fara and Flotta by arrangement.

MARWICK HEAD   OS 6

The promontory on the north-west coast, 2 miles south of Brough Head and generally acknowledged as one of the best sea bird cliffs in Orkney. Many thousands of birds can be seen and peregrines are regularly noted.

SUMMER: guillemot, razorbill, puffin, kittiwake, fulmar, shag, raven, peregrine.

Leave the A967 westwards, quarter of a mile north of its junction with A986. At B9056 turn right and first left to Mar Wick Bay. Walk along the cliffs northwards.

ROUSAY   OS 6

Rousay is one of the northern isles and is separated from the mainland by Eynhallow Sound. Its 6 miles by 4 miles is sufficient for a holiday and its cliffs and moorlands hold an interesting variety of species among which Arctic skua and hen harrier are outstanding.

SUMMER: guillemot, razorbill, puffin, kittiwake, fulmar, Arctic skua, hen harrier.

Rousay is reached by boats of the Orkney Islands Shipping Co. from Kirkwall. There are regular sailings and stops are made at Egilsay as well. Accommodation limited.

WESTRAY   OS 5

This is one of the largest of the northern isles and fortunately well populated by man and birds. Its cliffs hold sea birds and the hills Arctic and great skuas. No place in its 10 miles by 5 miles is further than a mile from the sea and it would take a good holiday to fully explore. There are large sandy beaches, fresh water lochs and it forms a convenient stepping off point for Papa Westray.

SUMMER: guillemot, razorbill, puffin, kittiwake, fulmar, raven, Arctic and great skuas.

The Orkney Islands Shipping Co. run a regular service almost every day in summer from Kirkwall.

Outer Hebrides

These islands lie at the north-western corner of Britain and stretch 130 miles from north to south. The coastline holds numbers of long sea lochs that stretch inland for several miles and the islands are divided by only shallow sandy straits. The geology of the Hebrides is of paramount importance to bird and human distribution. The western side of the group faces the open Atlantic and has received large deposits of shell sand. A glance at any map of the Uists shows the smooth and sand-strewn western coast and the rocky indented and sheltered eastern coast.

The western dunes have created a soil rich in lime giving rise to the characteristic sweet grass machair, and both weather

The Ultimate Challenge: these isolated islands are not all covered in this guide, but all are outstanding for birds. They hold the most elusive of all sea-birds, Leach's petrel, as well as gannets, storm petrels, and thousands (millions?) of auks. For the expedition minded they present the ultimate challenge of British ornithology

and man have carried seaweed on to the land and enriched it. This fertile area is in sharp contrast to the central and eastern peat ridden sections of the islands. The western side has farms with cattle and arable farming, the eastern has a mass of acid lochs and is mainly barren.

Birds are nowhere more plentiful than on the western cliffs, and the southern isles of Berneray and Mingulay are outstanding. The eastern sea lochs hold numbers of feeding divers and the sea is a favourite feeding ground of gannets. Golden eagle, buzzard, hen harrier, short-eared owl, raven and heron all breed amongst the peat of the interior where the outstanding species are skuas and greylag geese. The latter breed on Loch Druidibeg but move west on to the lochs of the machair with their young. These lochs shelter dunlin, duck and very rarely, red-necked phalarope, while the beaches hold oystercatchers, terns and ringed plovers.

For information contact Western Isles Tourist Association, 21 South Beach Street, Stornoway, who publish an official *Guide* at 2s. 6d., and *Where to Stay in the Western Isles,* also 2s. 6d.

THE FLANNAN ISLES OS 12

The Flannans lie 17 miles north-west of Gallan Head on the west side of Lewis, and consist of 7 islands and many skerries. The largest island, Eilean Mor, covers 39 acres, rises to 288 feet, and has a lighthouse. All of the isles are cliff bound. Leach's petrels breed abundantly, this being one of their five British breeding stations.

SUMMER: Leach's petrel, puffin, guillemot, razorbill, shag, kittiwake, fulmar, black guillemot, eider.

The end of June is the best time for a visit which will be a matter of arrangement and negotiation with previous visitors and the lighthouse authorities. The Scottish Ornithologists' Club is a good source of information.

LOCH DRUIDIBEG OS 23

The loch is in the northern half of South Uist near Howmore. It was declared a National Nature Reserve in 1958 and the Reserve now covers 4,145 acres of peat loch together with innumerable islands, machair, farmland and open sandy shore. It thus covers the full needs of the native greylag geese that are its principal attraction. Some 40–50 pairs breed annually and form the most important remaining colony in Britain. After the breeding season up to 300 geese congregate on the machair between Howmore and Eochar. The huge Loch Bee to the north is an important haunt of wildfowl in winter.

SUMMER: greylag goose, ringed plover, dunlin.

A permit is required to visit the Reserve in summer, and there is a small hostel attached to the Reserve at Grogany Lodge Annex. Inquiries for both should be addressed to The Warden, Stilligarry, Lochboisdale, South Uist.

ST. KILDA OS 17

St. Kilda stands 45 miles west of Griminish Point, North Uist, Outer Hebrides. There are seven islands and stacks in the group of which Hirta is the largest covering 1,575 acres and rising to a height of nearly 1,400 feet. The Ard Uachdarachd buttress of Conachair is the highest sea cliff in Britain, and the western face of Boreray rising to 1,250 feet is amongst the best cliffs for sea birds in the country. St. Kilda was inhabited until 1930 and has since 1957 been used as a radar station by the Army. It was made a National Nature Reserve when it was re-populated.

St. Kilda holds the largest gannetry in the world, a recent estimate showing 44,000 pairs. It also has large colonies of fulmar (20,000 on Hirta, perhaps 40,000 in the group), Leach's and storm petrels, and Manx shearwater all four of which breed on Carn More. The puffin is the commonest bird, but the other auks are quite numerous. The St. Kilda wren is unique and about 100 pairs breed on Hirta.

SUMMER: gannet, fulmar, Leach's and storm petrels, Manx shearwater, puffin, guillemot, razorbill, kittiwake, black guillemot, gulls, eider, St. Kilda wren.

Access is unrestricted but difficult. The National Trust for Scotland owns the group and organises expeditions periodically. The 'Island's Cruise' of that body calls at Hirta. All enquiries to the Nature Conservancy Scottish Office, 12 Hope Terrace, Edinburgh 7, or the Scottish National Trust, 5 Charlotte Square, Edinburgh 2.

SOUTH UIST   OS 23 and 32

The island is connected by causeways northwards to Benbecula (1939) and further north to North Uist (1960). The visitor can thus easily explore all three islands though it is likely that he will make this island his headquarters. Apart from Loch Druidibeg, which is treated separately, the lochs of the machair, moor and sea hold a rich variety of species including Arctic skua. The sands hold the usual summer species and a good selection of migrant and wintering waders. The promontory of Rudha Andvule and its lochan is an excellent spot at all seasons.

WINTER: white-fronted and barnacle geese, bar-tailed godwit, sanderling.

SPRING: whimbrel, turnstone, purple sandpiper.

SUMMER: Arctic skua, black-throated diver, eider, merganser, Arctic tern, dunlin, ringed plover.

AUTUMN: waders, gannet.

Accommodation is available in Lochboisdale and in private homes in other parts of the island, see *Where to stay in the Western Isles*.

The RSPB opened a new reserve at Balranald, North Uist, in 1967. Birds include red-necked phalarope, other waders, gulls, three species of tern, eight species of duck including eider and wigeon, and corncrake. Permits are not required but visitors are asked to contact the warden at Hougharry.

STORNOWAY HARBOUR AND LOCH BRANAHUIE

OS 8

The Stornoway area is not only convenient of access but also has a wide variety of habitat. The woods are dealt with separately and we are here concerned with the water and muddy, rocky edges of the harbour and with the small Loch Branahuie lying on the isthmus that connects the Eye Peninsula to the mainland. The Iceland gull is a regular winter visitor to the harbour and is commoner than the glaucous which also occurs. In spring the scoter and velvet scoter that winter in the bay to the north are joined by up to 500 long-tailed duck.

WINTER: merganser, long-tailed duck, scoter, velvet scoter, Iceland and glaucous gulls, turnstone, purple sandpiper.

The harbour is the town centre. Loch Branahuie lies 3 miles east on the A866.

STORNOWAY WOODS   OS 8

The woods form part of the castle grounds, now belonging to the people of Stornoway. Though not the only trees in the Outer Hebrides the nearest comparable woodland is 40 miles to the east. The bird population is one of the most outstanding in the Outer Hebrides.

SUMMER: wood pigeon, rook, blue tit, treecreeper, robin, whitethroat, chiffchaff, goldcrest, tree sparrow, buzzard, corncrake, raven, hooded crow, dipper, grey wagtail.

Access direct from Stornoway.

Shetland Isles

The Shetlands lie in latitude 60° north, which is the same as Cape Farewell in Greenland and 6° south of the Arctic circle. They extend for 70 miles from north to south, and 37 from east to west. The mainland occupies about two-thirds of the total area but the coast is so indented that no place is more than 3 miles from the sea. Only nineteen of the hundred odd islands are now inhabited and the mainland has over half the population of 17,000. Every one of these islands is good for birds and choice is limited by ease of access, and time available. If, amongst so many wonderful places, some can be said to be outstanding, they are Noss, Fetlar and Hermaness, and the intending visitor should try to include at least one of these in his travels.

Shetland is a rugged land which fact is belied by the modest maximum height of 1,475 feet. It is essentially igneous in geology and its mantle is rough grass underlain by a thick layer of peat. Only Fetlar and the southern half of Unst have a semblance of green fields and pasture.

For information and accommodation contact the Shetland Tourist Association, Information Centre, Alexandra Wharf, Lerwick.

The RSPB representative is R. J. Tulloch, Reafirth, Mid Yell; and he knows what is happening in every part of the islands.

FAIR ISLE   OS 4

Fair Isle is 24 miles south-west of Sumburgh Head between the Orkneys and the Shetlands and is completely isolated. Its 'drawing power' is thus very high though its geographical position is off the main migration routes. It is not a mere speck in the ocean, being 3 miles by 1 mile, and has some of the finest cliff scenery in Britain; it supports a crofting population of over forty. Eagle Clarke's pioneer studies put Fair Isle on the ornithological map in 1912 and it has retained its pre-eminence ever since. After the last war the island was purchased by George Waterston and the Bird Observatory was opened with Kenneth Williamson as the first Warden. The National Trust for Scotland purchased the Isle in 1954, and Peter Davis became Warden in 1957. Roy Dennis took over in 1963. Though Fair Isle is a migration study post it does have an interesting variety of breeding species. Vagrants occur every week of the autumn season and up till 1963, 17 species had been added to the British List from their occurrence on this tiny island. In 1964 the following 'rare' birds were recorded on the island: short-toed lark (3), black-eared wheatear (2), great reed warbler, subalpine warbler, Arctic warbler (4), Richard's pipit (several), citrine wagtail, steppe grey shrike, serin, scarlet grosbeak (several), rustic bunting (2), and little bunting, plus a whole range of the more usual barred warblers, bluethroats and Lapland buntings. Anything can turn up. A brand new observatory will be opened in 1969.

SPRING: migrants, shrikes, rarities.

SUMMER: great and Arctic skuas, guillemot, razorbill, puffin, storm petrel, kittiwake, fulmar, wren (Fair Isle subspecies), twite.

AUTUMN: migrants, rarities, short-toed lark, barred warbler, bluethroat, vagrants.

The *Good Shepherd* runs between Grutness, Sumburgh, Shetland and Fair Isle twice weekly in summer, at 21s. 6d. return. It is thus convenient for Sumburgh Airport and the south, though visitors may boat to Lerwick. Accommodation is available at 21s. to 30s. per day full board and is less primitive than most observatories. Full details from The Warden, Fair Isle Bird Observatory, by Lerwick, Shetland; and between 1st December and 31st March from the Hon. Sec., 21 Regent Terrace, Edinburgh 7.

FETLAR   OS 1

This is the smallest of the main islands and is often called the green island because of its fields and cultivation which make it unique in Shetland. It has breeding Manx shearwaters and storm petrels, Arctic and great skuas, and around the cliffs the usual birds are found in large colonies.

SUMMER: great and Arctic skuas, storm petrel, Manx shearwater, wigeon, golden plover, dunlin, snipe, auks, kittiwake.

There is a regular boat service from Lerwick and cottage accommodation is available.

MAINLAND   OS 1, 2, 3 and 4

The Mainland of Shetland is 33 miles long and an outstanding bird haunt in its own right. The visitor arriving for a trip to Hermaness and seeing gannets diving in Lerwick Harbour would be foolish not to explore further. Had he arrived in winter the same site would provide glaucous gull. A short exploration to Weisdale Voe in summer would produce both species of scoter (one breeding) and perhaps Unst would have to wait.

There are innumerable cliffs with breeding auks and kittiwakes. Arctic skuas breed in several places and great skuas are spreading from their northern strongholds. In winter interesting species include a variety of sea duck, glaucous gull, great northern diver and wild swans. During migration periods almost anything may turn up almost anywhere.

WINTER: divers, scoter, velvet scoter, long-tailed duck, eider, merganser, glaucous gull.

SUMMER: guillemot, razorbill, black guillemot, kittiwake, fulmar, raven, hooded crow, twite, wren, eider, merganser, scoter, gannet, divers, curlew, dunlin, common sandpiper, skuas, common and Arctic terns.

AUTUMN: waders, sea birds, passerines, rarities.

Amongst many sites worth a visit are Weisdale and Whiteness Voes, Walls and Ronas Hill National Nature Reserve. For
details of accommodation write to Shetland Tourist Association, Alexandra Wharf, Lerwick.

The North of Scotland and Orkney and Shetland Shipping
Co. Ltd., Matthews' Quay, Aberdeen, run a twice weekly service
from Aberdeen to Lerwick via Kirkwall, Orkney, leaving Tues-
day and Friday p.m. Ships may be joined one day earlier at
Leith. A direct overnight service from Aberdeen to Lerwick
leaves on Monday and Thursday p.m. BEA run daily air services to Sumburgh from Kirkwall, Aberdeen and Wick, with
connections to other parts of Britain.

NOSS   OS 3
Noss lies 3 miles east of Lerwick and its eastern cliffs drop
almost 600 feet to the sea. It is an outstanding sea bird colony
made all the more attractive by its convenient situation and the
fact that it is best seen from a boat. Over 3,000 pairs of gannets were counted in 1949, and the colony has probably grown
since. A large assembly of eiders congregate in the Noup of
Noss in late summer and both skuas breed.

SUMMER: gannet, guillemot, razorbill, puffin, black guillemot, kittiwake, eider, great and Arctic skuas.

Frequent tourist trips by boat from Lerwick around the
island. Alternatively cross from Lerwick to Bressay then walk
or taxi $2\frac{1}{2}$ miles to Noss Sound and summon the shepherd who
summers on Noss to row you across.

UNST   OS 1
Unst is 12 miles by 5 miles and is the most northerly island of
Britain. The southern half is well cultivated and the village of
Baltasound is quite sizeable by local standards. The cliff
scenery has been described as amongst the finest in the country,
culminating in the cliffs of Hermaness. Only a few stacks stretch
further northwards to Muckle Flugga with its lighthouse and
Out Stack the most northern rock of Britain.

At Hermaness the cliff tops are honeycombed with the burrows of puffins while on the cliffs themselves is a truly
magnificent gathering of sea birds. These species breed right
round the headland and on to the cliffs along Burra Firth. Both
Arctic and great skuas breed on the moorland and have
increased under protection to such an extent that the bonxie
has been able to spread from what was once almost its last
stand. Gannets have bred since 1917 on the offshore stacks and
skerries and are now firmly established and easily seen. All

of these marine species regularly flight to the freshwater of the Loch of Cliff which is separated from Burra Firth by only a narrow strip of land.

WINTER: whooper swan, eider, long-tailed duck, divers.

SUMMER: guillemot, razorbill, puffin, black guillemot, kittiwake, fulmar, Arctic and great skuas, gannet, whimbrel.

Baltasound is in regular steamer contact with Lerwick. The ferries between the Mainland and Yell, and Yell and Unst, provide an overland route. The Hermaness Reserve established in 1955 covers 2,383 acres but there are no restrictions on access. Full details are available from the Nature Conservancy Scottish Office.

YELL OS 1

Yell is the second largest of the Shetlands, 17 miles by 6 miles, and is the least visited by outsiders. It is a land of moor, rough grass and peat and though it has some magnificent cliffs, especially on the western coast, its main attractions lie inland. Whale Firth on the west and Mid-Yell Voe in the east almost cut the island in half and the village of Mid Yell forms an admirable centre.

Of many places to go the following areas contain most of the typical species: the ridge of Alin Knowes and, to the northwest, the deserted crofting area of Lumbister which has been described as the loveliest place in Yell. Both species of skua breed on the rising ground to the north of Loch of Lumbister and on the Whale Firth Peninsula.

SUMMER: great and Arctic skuas, kittiwake, guillemot, razorbill.

There are two main routes to Yell by sea from Lerwick to Mid Yell or 'overland'. The overland route leaves Lerwick by road to Mossbank where passengers are ferried across Yell sound to Ulsta. The route continues by road to Mid Yell.

INDEX OF PLACES